The Man Who Ran Faster Than Everyone

The Man Who Ran Faster Than Everyone

The Story of Tom Longboat

JACK BATTEN

Tundra Books

Copyright © 2002 by Jack Batten
Published in Canada by Tundra Books,
481 University Avenue, Toronto, Ontario M5G 2E9
Published in the United States by Tundra Books of Northern New York,
P.O. Box 1030, Plattsburgh, New York 12901
Library of Congress Control Number: 2001095369

National Library of Canada Cataloguing in Publication Data

Batten, Jack, 1932–
The man who ran faster than everyone : the story of Tom Longboat

Includes index.
ISBN 0-88776-507-6

1. Longboat, Tom, 1887-1949. 2. Runners (Sports)–Canada–Biography.
3. Indians of North America–Canada–Biography.
I. Title.

GV1061.15.L65B38 2002   796.42'4'092   C2001-902805-9

We acknowledge the support of the Canada Council for the Arts and the Ontario Arts
Council for our publishing program.

We acknowledge the financial support of the Government of Canada through the
Book Publishing Industry Development Program for our publishing activities.

Design: Blaine Herrmann

Printed and bound in Canada

1   2   3   4   5   6   07   06   05   04   03   02

For T. Gardiner Frayne,
a great writer and a great friend

Contents

Author's Note

When Tom Longboat and his fellow runners competed in races in the early years of the 20th century, they ran at distances measured in miles, yards, and feet. The marathon, for example, was 26 miles, 385 yards. In metric terms, the marathon measures at 42.2 kilometers. In this book, the imperial measurement – miles, yards, and feet – is used in order to conform to the standards of Longboat's day. To convert the imperial measurement to metric terms, use the following table.

One mile = 1.6093 kilometers

One yard = 0.9144 meters

One foot = 0.3048 meters

One inch = 2.54 centimeters

CHAPTER ONE

The Best Runner in the World

To us, today, the race seems peculiar. It consisted of two fit young men running around the small track at Madison Square Garden in New York City 262 times. This event took place on the night of December 15, 1908, and it involved the two competitors circling the track time after time to cover the marathon distance of 26 miles, 385 yards (42.2 kilometers). With about four laps to go, one of the two – Dorando Pietri of Italy – pitched forward on his face, barely conscious and unable to muster one more step. The other runner, close to exhaustion, struggled on alone over the rest of the distance. When he crossed the finish line, he had been running for 2 hours, 45 minutes, and 5.2 seconds, and he won a prize of $3,750. The victorious runner was Tom Longboat of Canada.

For sports fans of the present, accustomed to quick, busy, high-energy action, more attuned to team games than individual contests, the race at the Garden comes across as the athletic equivalent of watching paint dry. But in the early years of the 20th century, such events as the Tom Longboat-Dorando Pietri race were all the rage. Fourteen thousand roaring spectators packed the Garden to cheer the runners that night, and hundreds more – unable to buy a ticket for the sold-out event – milled in the streets outside, impatient to learn the race's outcome.

Toronto Reference Library

🥾 Twenty-one and dapper, this is Tom Longboat on the eve of his first great professional victory over Italy's Dorando Pietri at the marathon distance in New York's Madison Square Garden in December 1908.

These fans, unlike today's, preferred man-on-man rivalries to team sports, and they applauded endurance over style. They flocked to thirty-round boxing matches, two-mile single-scull rowing events, and, above all, to long-distance running races. There was a craze in North America for distance running in the years before World War I, and two-man races, like the one on the night of December 15, 1908, were the centerpieces of the sport's enormous popularity. In the winters, these races were held in indoor arenas and in military armories. In the summers, they switched to large open-air stadiums, two-man competitions at such venues as the Polo Grounds in New York and the Hanlan's Point Stadium on the Toronto Islands. More conventional distance events figured into the racing mix too; these were usually marathons featuring fields of many competitors running over roads on the outskirts of a city and into the downtown core. Spectators lined the streets and cheered themselves hoarse for the runners, especially for Tom Longboat.

In the age of the long-distance runner, Longboat was the greatest of them all. He won more races than any of his contemporaries, and he triumphed at every distance from three miles to the marathon. He seemed almost super-humanly tireless, ready to run any race at any time. In the six weeks after his 1908 victory over Dorando Pietri, he ran two more indoor marathons — one in Buffalo, the other back in Madison Square Garden. Longboat won both, and as if to show how secure he felt about winning, he took a few days off between races to get married and take part in a wedding reception for hundreds of guests at Toronto's Massey Hall.

Longboat's running feats made him by far the best-known Canadian abroad during the first two decades of the 20th century and the most popular Canadian at home. His fellow citizens couldn't get enough of Tom Longboat. On an autumn Saturday in the first year of his growing celebrity, 1907, he set off on an exhibition solo run — who could imagine such a thing today? — that covered 35 miles from the city of Hamilton, east along Lakeshore Road, to the center of Toronto. Nearing the Humber River three-quarters of the way through the run, Longboat developed severe foot blisters and limped into an accompanying automobile. The police were horrified by Longboat's withdrawal from the run. One hundred thousand of his fans had gathered along the route at the Toronto end, anxious for a glimpse of their hero. The police feared a riot if all that rewarded the people's wait was a shadowy Longboat in the rear of a Model T. They pleaded with him to return to his run, just for the last mile. Longboat obliged.

It's difficult to measure such an entity as public adulation, but Longboat was probably as idolized in his time as Wayne Gretzky was in his. Glory and grace touched both men in their different athletic performances, and fans responded to each with equal degrees of helpless admiration. Both men seemed accessible and friendly; nothing stuck-up about Tom or Wayne. And, in a satisfying coincidence, both came from the same part of the world – Gretzky from the town of Brantford in Southern Ontario, and Longboat from the gently rolling countryside immediately to the town's southeast.

But it isn't helpful to pursue the Longboat-Gretzky comparison to its limits because one unbridgeable divide separates the two men: Gretzky is white while Longboat was Native. The gently rolling land where Longboat grew up was an Indian reserve, the Six Nations. It was a place where many people lived in drafty shacks, rarely earned a white man's wage, had bad teeth, and died young. Natives made up Canada's underclass, Longboat included, and no matter how much adoration the public heaped on him as an athlete, Longboat was never allowed to forget what he was and where he came from.

All he had to do, if he needed reminding, was look in the daily news-papers. Sportswriters routinely identified him by such insulting terms as "the Redskin," "Heap Big Chief," and "the Injun." The *Globe* once pointed out, with apparently no conscious racial sneer intended, that Longboat possessed only "the light veneer of the white man's ways."

Longboat was a Native, and it cost him. After his death in 1948, he was quoted by one of his sons as having advised years earlier: "Don't go into running. There's no money in it." Longboat was wrong; there was very good money in running, just not for him. The white men who managed Longboat's career and promoted his races were mostly well-to-do business-men before their associations with Longboat, and they were measurably more well-to-do after the associations ended. But the money Longboat earned with his magnificent running never seemed to stick to his own fingers. And after his retirement from racing, the best job he ever found was with Toronto's City Street Cleaning Department. From 1927 to 1944,

Longboat picked up garbage from the streets where his fellow citizens had once cheered him to the skies.

Longboat was never known to express bitterness or regret over his fate, at least not when a reporter with a pencil was around to record his reflections. Longboat left the impression, which was surely true in large part, that the running itself brought him pride and satisfaction. He found joy in running. He loved to run as a boy, and when he became an elderly man, he loved equally to set off on long walking rambles. In his final three years, ill with diabetes and living once more on the Six Nations reserve, he used to hike from his home to the town of Hagersville several times a week, each walk adding up to a round trip of 20 happy miles.

Running was what defined Longboat to himself. He was a good husband and father, a diligent worker, an amiable and gentle man, but most of all, he was a runner. He rejoiced in running, and for a long and significant period when distance running was the king of sports, Tom Longboat was the best runner in the world.

CHAPTER TWO

Beginnings

Many years after the fact, Longboat put his finger on the humble event that got his life launched on its course to unexpected fame. This event, Longboat recollected, took place at the beginning of the lacrosse season when he was 17, which would put it in the early spring of 1905. Young Tom, a member of the Onondaga nation, played for the Onondaga team in a Six Nations league. North American Natives had invented the sport of lacrosse centuries before white people arrived.

In the sport's earliest times, teams made up of dozens – even hundreds – of players competed against one another in games that lasted for days on fields that were six times the size of a modern football field. These games were seen by the North American Natives to have spiritual elements, and were often played as a curing ritual for sick or injured people. White settlers took up their own version of lacrosse, which was streamlined with far fewer players and a much smaller playing area in accordance with rules developed in 1867 by a Montreal dentist named William George Beers. The game became Canada's most popular team sport, until hockey displaced it, and it was this modern version of lacrosse that was eventually adopted by the Natives in the late 19th century.

🏃 Longboat's first sport, lacrosse, was a favorite among most young men on the Six Nations reserve, and he played on a team like the one shown above.

Tom Longboat was known as a lacrosse player who could cover the ground in a hurry. A teammate, who thought he was something of a speed merchant himself, challenged Tom to a race in the spring of 1905 – just the two of them, up and down the reserve roads. Longboat couldn't recall later the length of the race. *Two miles, or maybe three?* All Longboat knew for certain, all that really mattered to the story and to Longboat's future as a runner, was that he left the other boy in the dust both literally and metaphorically.

Intrigued and encouraged by this result, a few weeks later Longboat entered the Victoria Day race in the neighboring town of Caledonia. Like most Ontario small towns, Caledonia celebrated Queen Victoria's birthday on May 24 with a fair that included as a feature attraction a hotly waged running race for the local men, both white and Native.

Longboat began the race at the same pace as he began the contest against his lacrosse buddy: very fast. *Get out front early and stay there.* A flaw in this strategy ultimately emerged. The race was five miles long – farther than Longboat had ever run at top speed in one consecutive stretch – and in the fifth mile, he began to fade. One runner passed him. Longboat held on for second place. Not bad, Longboat thought, but he wondered what first place would feel like. He resolved to prepare better for the next year's Victoria Day race.

From childhood on, Longboat had always run. But it wasn't with any particular discipline, never with competition in mind. Now, spurred by the thought of the future May 24 race in Caledonia, he imposed some organization on his running. Nothing rigid, just a way of training with a vague method behind it. In this, he got help from a man named Bill Davis, who had excellent running credentials. Davis was a Mohawk who lived in the principal Six Nations community of Oshwegan, and in 1901, he finished second in the most significant long-distance race in North America – the Boston Marathon.

Longboat absorbed the wisdom that Davis offered, ideas that originated in the larger world of competitive racing beyond the Six Nations. Then he improvised on these lessons with his own small variations, and in the process, he arrived at a rough set of training techniques that seemed congenial to his body and its needs.

Using the reserve roads as a measuring device, he ran for gradually lengthened distances. Three reserve roads one week, four reserve roads the next, then five, six. He alternated tough training runs with more leisurely trots; a hard session followed by an easy session. *Allow the muscles to build strength gradually and surely. Develop the mechanism for taking deep and sustained breaths.* Then he set aside periods for complete rest – time to let the muscles and breathing apparatus relax.

And sometimes Longboat threw crazy stunts into the running routine. One day, he walked and ran all the way to the town of Dunnville and back. "Holy mackerel," people exclaimed, "fifty miles!" Longboat thought it was a lark. Another time, an older relative went off by horse and buggy to visit a friend 40 miles away in Hamilton. Tom gave the relative a half-hour head start, then put his feet on the same route. He beat the horse-drawn buggy to the friend's house. Admittedly, the horse was an elderly nag, but Longboat's run was still an impressive feat.

All of this running, Longboat realized, brought pleasure. He liked the brush of the wind on his face as he ran. He liked the sensation in the workings of his leg muscles. He took satisfaction in all of the physical reactions of his body. There was a mental component to running's positives too — Longboat appreciated the way running emptied his mind of his worries. And for a young man not yet out of adolescence, Longboat had accumulated more than his fair burden of woes, even by the standards of the often grim existence on Indian reserves at the turn of the century.

The Six Nations, which the reserve of that name included, were the Onondaga, Mohawk, Oneida, Seneca, Cayuga, and Tuscarora. Their ancestors had lived for millennia on the rich and graceful land south of the St. Lawrence River and Lakes Ontario and Erie. In the 14th century, five of the Six Nations — all except the Tuscarora, who were based in an area farther south and connected with the others later — joined in a political institution called the Iroquois Confederacy, made up principally of resourceful agricultural communities. This union took place less than a couple of centuries before Jacques Cartier's voyages from France up the St. Lawrence signalled that Europeans were moving into the Native world.

Once the white men arrived, the Iroquois peoples showed themselves adept at trading and bartering with the newcomers. But their talent was only prolonging the inevitable — the whites wanted land to expand into, and the Six Nations were sitting on prime property. The defining event was the American War of Independence in 1776. Most of the Six Nations made the mistake of backing the British, and when the thirteen American colonies won the war, the Natives' days in Upper New York State and Pennsylvania were numbered.

The Six Nations had the advantage of a leader, Joseph Brant, who had been educated in white schools and had embraced Christianity. He was just the sort of Native whom the British wished all Natives to be like. Brant helped to negotiate a deal with the British in 1784, in which nearly 2,000 people from all six Iroquois nations moved north across the border to a large and empty parcel of land on the Grand River in Upper Canada. What the British liked about the arrangement was that it kept all these annoying Natives in one place. To Christian whites, Natives were heathen and lackadaisical. As far as Natives were concerned, white society was too quick and regimented, too obsessed with materialistic ambition. But whites had the numbers, money, and power, and the Six Nations found themselves – an independent and productive people for generations – now confined on a reserve where, through the last decades of the 19th century, many of them began a slide into poverty, despair, alcoholism, and suicide.

This terrible process was ingrained at the time Tom Longboat drew his first breath – born Thomas Charles Longboat (along with his Iroquois name, Cogwagee, which roughly translates as "Everything") on June 4, 1887, to his parents, George and Betsy, on the Six Nations reserve. The records aren't clear on the number of Longboat children; there were probably four – two

Archives of Ontario

 Joseph Brant was the Mohawk chief who played a large role in bringing 2,000 members of the Six Nations from their original lands in Upper New York State to their new home on the reserve near Brantford, Ontario in the late 18th century.

girls and two boys – with Tom the second youngest, senior only to his brother, Simon. Like most of the Onondaga, the Longboats lived in the eastern or downriver part of the reserve. Home to the family was isolated deep in the bush, a cabin made of rough logs, mortar filling in the crevices. The cabin measured about 18 feet long by 14 feet wide, and inside it consisted of one room with three beds, a woodstove for heat, two coal oil lamps for light. George Longboat worked a piece of surrounding land that was too barren to call a farm. It supported a cow, a few chickens, marginally more rabbits, a patchy garden of vegetables, and no horse for ploughing. The family barely kept its head above water.

Things got worse when Tom was five years old; his father died. At about the same time, his older siblings began to move out into the world, leaving Tom and Simon alone with their mother. Life must have moved with too much random suddenness for little Tom.

At home and in social settings, the Longboats and almost everybody they knew spoke Onondaga. It was the language of religious ceremonies at the Onondaga longhouse, which was a combined community center and spiritual headquarters. Tom switched to English mainly for his education at the small school on the reserve. There wasn't much education though for Tom, who had to stay home many days to help his mother and to look after his little brother.

In the fall when Tom was 12, life threw him another curve, one that he might have seen coming. In 1879, the Canadian federal government had arrived at a scheme for turning heathen Native children into a semblance of Christian boys and girls; they removed them from the reserves and, in the expectation of creating thousands of little Joseph and Josephine Brants, they drilled them in white man's ways at church-run boarding schools designed specifically for Native children. It was a well-meant plan in theory, but too often in practice, it turned out to be horribly cruel. Generations of Native youth were left baffled and lonely in their growing years, separated from home, family, reserve, and everything else that gave them their cultural identity.

Archives of Ontario

👟 This idyllic drive is deceptive. It leads the way to the Mohawk Institute, an Anglican mission school for Native children, which Longboat, 12 years old, found so oppressive that he ran away from it after a few months, never to receive further formal education.

In September 1899, one more in a long line of displaced kids, Tom Longboat found himself at the Mohawk Institute – an Anglican mission school for Indians in Brantford. He hated it. There were rules, almost all of them beginning with a negative: no Onondaga language, no Indian religion. Speak English, worship the Christian god. Go to class in the morning; go to bed in the evening. Everything by the clock. Back home on the reserve Tom knew, a boy could sit with his friends, talk, listen, repair a lacrosse stick, gaze at the horizon, wait for the sunset. A day well spent, all activities equal in value. At the mission school, such conduct would rate another name: laziness. Tom was caught in a clash of cultures. He decided to run away from the Mohawk Institute.

The first time he lit out, in the spring of 1900, Tom made a mistake – he went home to his mother, where the Institute officials easily found him. That landed Tom back in school. The second time he fled, a few weeks later, he hid at an uncle's house, the home of his namesake, the senior Tom

Longboat. The officials didn't think to look for Tom there and soon forgot about him altogether. Whether he realized it or not, Tom, still only 12, with only the most basic education, had reached the end of his childhood.

As a teenager, Tom took up the labor of his late father – he coaxed a living from the stingy Longboat soil. At harvest time, on the flourishing farms outside the reserve, he earned a few dollars picking apples and gathering corn. Then he walked beyond the farms to Burlington and other towns with canning factories, where he hired on for a few weeks' work, stuffing fruit and vegetables into tin cans for sale in stores.

It was small wonder that Tom found so much pleasure in running. The simple physical act came as a huge relief from the rest of his hard days. Tom ran and trained, forgot his troubles, grew stronger and faster. His dedicated regimen must have been ready to tell him something about his running talent. The Victoria Day fair in Caledonia rolled around in May 1906, and Tom once more entered the five-mile race. This time, there was no fading in the fifth mile, no loss of stamina, no slowing down. This time, Tom made a joke of the competition. He finished so far in front of the other runners that people at the fair had to laugh. "That Indian boy," they said between chuckles, "that Tom Longboat, he's one heck of a runner."

Bill Davis thought so. He told young Tom that he should aim higher; he should move up to a more demanding level of competition. Tom seemed reluctant to take this next big step, but Davis persisted. He had a particular race in mind for Tom – the *Hamilton Herald* Around the Bay Race. It was an annual event that attracted a superior caliber of runner. Davis said Tom was ready for the race. He said Tom had the speed and grit to take on the best runners in the entire country.

CHAPTER THREE

In the Running

Hamilton, down the highway from the Six Nations and already a booming steel city, happened to be a hotbed of long-distance running. The first Canadians ever to enter the Boston Marathon, in the race of 1900, were Jack Caffery, Bill Sherring, and Frank Hughson. They finished first, second, and third. All three were from Hamilton. Caffery won again the following year in the race where Bill Davis finished second. In the summer of 1906, Bill Sherring entered the marathon at the Olympic Games.

Canada's Sports Hall of Fame

🥾 When Bill Sherring of Hamilton, Ontario won the marathon at the 1906 Olympic Games in Athens, his victory propelled distance running to new heights of popularity in Canada. Crown Prince Constantine of Greece enthusiastically accompanies Sherring in the race's last few yards.

The Olympics took place every four years. There was one in St. Louis, Missouri in 1904, and there was another scheduled for London, England in 1908. But for the only time in Olympic history, an extra Games were staged in Athens, Greece in 1906. This event was referred to as the Intercalated Games, and Bill Sherring of Hamilton won the marathon – a victory that greatly enhanced the event's popularity among Canadians.

The local Hamilton race that was the biggest attraction on the yearly running calendar was sponsored by a newspaper, the *Hamilton Herald*, and its course took it in a loop around Burlington Bay. Hence, its name: the *Hamilton Herald* Around the Bay Race. The event, which was founded in 1894, began and ended in front of the *Herald* offices, and in between, it weaved through the city's east end, over the sand dunes of the bay, then west and back to the city past a couple of Hamilton landmarks – the Royal Botanical Gardens and Dundurn Castle. The complete distance was 19 miles and 168 yards, and the race took place in early October of each year.

In 1906, the year when Tom Longboat listened to Bill Davis's urgings and signed up for the race, the field numbered 26 competitors, and the favorite to win, in the absence that year of entries by Sherring and Caffery, was John Marsh. He was an Englishman who had won many important races in his homeland, then emigrated to the Canadian West, where he ran with distinction for the *Telegram* Amateur Athletic Club of Winnipeg. The term "favorite" as applied to Marsh wasn't just a figure of speech. Gambling on races constituted one of the major appeals for spectators at long-distance running events, and the Around the Bay Race was no exception. Dozens of men, perhaps hundreds, gathered at the race's starting point an hour or two early, in plenty of time to check out the field and place their wagers with the bookmakers on the scene, who set the odds. To both bettors and bookies, John Marsh was the overwhelming choice for the 1906 event.

At the starting line, Longboat hardly cut a figure that struck fear into the hearts of the other runners, or tempted the gamblers to lay a big buck on Longboat to win. He looked gawky, younger than his nineteen years; gangly, even though he wasn't particularly tall – five-foot-ten – and 140 pounds.

And his clothing marked him as poor and unaware of racing fashion: a cheap cotton bathing suit instead of running shorts, a floppy jersey, and worn canvas shoes.

Despite his appearance and youth, despite his status as an unknown quantity, a few bettors took a chance on Longboat. One man identified only as J. Yaldon, acting out of a sense of fun, made a wager with a bookie, $1,000 to $2. Yaldon laid down the two bucks on condition that, if Longboat miraculously won, the bookie owed him the thousand. A couple of other bookmakers accepted the same sort of long-shot bets on Longboat.

Once the race began, Longboat's running form was notable mostly for its unorthodoxy. His stride was low, his feet rising only fractionally off the ground, and he carried his hands similarly low, at hip level. It was actually an intelligent style, economical and energy-saving, but it made Longboat stand out among his more high-stepping opponents in a way that not many of the spectators entirely approved of.

To everybody's surprise, the odd-looking boy stayed with the leaders as the miles clicked by. In fact, by the 14-mile mark, the only man in front of Longboat was the favorite, Marsh. The two of them seemed to have a little personal game going. Longboat would tuck in just behind Marsh for a quarter mile, then spurt up, pass Marsh, and stick in front for a hundred yards. Marsh would smile patiently and wait until Longboat's burst of exuberance wore off and he slowed back to Marsh's side. This happened four or five times, but the game within the race did nothing to persuade the spectators, or Marsh, that Longboat was an authentic threat to an eventual Marsh victory.

That perception changed with a little under four miles left in the race. This was the point where the runners climbed up the steep hill from Burlington Beach and turned along Stone Road to head home. The natural temptation, after the demanding climb, was to slow down, even if briefly, and take a little off the pace in order to gather oneself for the final charge. Marsh yielded to the temptation. He slowed. Longboat didn't. He bolted to the lead, and no matter how frantically Marsh pursued Longboat, he couldn't catch the apparently more fit and determined teenage opponent. Only one glitch marred Longboat's performance: with less than a mile to go, he took a wrong turn on the course and covered a wasted 75 yards before the spectators got him back on track. Even then, by the end of the race — a glorious end for Longboat — he had stretched his lead over Marsh to almost three minutes and was all alone in first place.

J. Yaldon was ecstatic. He won $1,000. The bookmakers were appalled. One reported that Longboat's victory cost him $4,000. Everyone who gathered at the finish line was flabbergasted at the unknown runner who had taken first place, but nobody was more surprised than a man named Harry Rosenthal.

Rosenthal was from Toronto, where he worked as a bookbinder at W. J. Gage & Co., publisher and dealer in wholesale books and stationery. In his spare time, Rosenthal was a devoted running fan, an expert at sizing up and handicapping runners. He liked to hang out with the runners, attend their races, bet money on the result. When it came to running, Harry Rosenthal was a very serious man, and he made up his mind on the spot at the Around the Bay Race that, in Longboat, he was looking at a runner of great promise and that he must get himself a piece of the amazing Onondaga teenager.

Rosenthal sought out Longboat and laid his cards on the table: he, Rosenthal, would sign on as the manager that Longboat didn't have but needed. Rosenthal explained that Longboat, an amateur, could accept no payment for winning races, but Rosenthal would arrange the minimal expense money that Longboat was permitted, would enter him in races, book transportation and accommodation, and generally relieve Longboat of the petty details of everything except the actual running of the races.

What was in it for Rosenthal? For one thing, it would entitle him to bragging rights if his man, Longboat, was the champ that Rosenthal expected him to be. More materially, Rosenthal would profit from placing bets on

Longboat and collecting the winnings. He might even slip Longboat a few bucks under the table if Longboat kept quiet about it.

Now, Rosenthal asked point-blank: what did Longboat think of the proposal?

Against all odds in his difficult life, Longboat had remained a genial and civil young man. He rarely said no to anything that was asked of him. With Rosenthal, Longboat felt both pleased and intimidated that this fast-talking gent from the big city held such a high opinion of his athletic talents. Maybe Longboat glimpsed something better for himself in the immediate future — something away from the hardships of the Six Nations, something that his running might promise. Out of these assorted impulses and motives, Longboat told Rosenthal that he was game for whatever Rosenthal had in mind. Rosenthal said what he had in mind, for starters, was a relocation for Longboat from the Six Nations to Toronto.

Toronto was then a city of 200,000 citizens. It was a city of redbrick houses with gingerbread trim, a metropolis with streetcars that clattered on tracks down the middle of most major thoroughfares. The streetcars carried workers to their jobs in the big farm implement factory in the west end, to the equally large hog-butchering business on Front Street (a business that got the city its enduring label, "Hogtown"), to the hundreds of other thriving enterprises that Toronto boasted. The city was fast developing into the leading industrial, commercial, and financial center in the country. The bosses who grew wealthy from the profitable businesses – the Masseys (farm implements), Joseph Flavelle (hogs), Timothy Eaton (department store) – were scrupulous about giving back to the community in the form of concert halls and hospitals, the Art Gallery of Ontario, the University of Toronto. They also contributed to the building of many houses of worship, reflecting the city's overwhelmingly British heritage: Anglican churches, Presbyterian, Methodist, churches that inspired another lasting nickname, "Toronto the Good."

Longboat was stunned by his first extended exposure to Toronto, so bustling, crowded, and ambitious; so pious and churchgoing; so opposite to the relatively more relaxed, country calm of the reserve. But Harry Rosenthal eased the adjustment.

Rosenthal, a bachelor, lived with his widowed mother, Emma, on Regent Street in the workingman's Cabbagetown neighborhood. He gave Longboat a bed at his place, and he spoke to his boss at the Gage company, General Manager William Gundy, about a job for Longboat. Gundy hired young Tom as an office boy. The work was simple enough – delivering messages, packing books in boxes – but Longboat found the job oppressive. It was an indoor occupation, indoors at Gage's cramped offices on lower Spadina Avenue, and Longboat felt uncomfortable away from his accustomed outdoors life.

Nevertheless, he stuck it out as Gage's office boy, partially because William Gundy didn't mind when Longboat took days off to train. Longboat needed to stay in shape because Harry Rosenthal hustled him into his next race, the Ward Marathon, less than two weeks after his arrival in town.

John Ward was one of a kind: a tailor, a socialist, an elected member of Toronto City Council, and a civic-minded sponsor of sporting events, all of which he named after himself. The Ward Marathon was set at 15 miles (meaning it fell far short of legitimate marathon length). Beginning at the foot of High Park, it followed a route that guaranteed that no runner would lose his way – west on Lakeshore Road, turn around and east on Lakeshore, seven and a half miles out the dirt road and the same in.

The 1906 event attracted 73 entrants, with Longboat, based on his dramatic performance in the Around the Bay Race, installed as the betting favorite. From the start, he made the oddsmakers look smart: he easily held the early lead, challenged only by a young man named Bill Cumming, who represented the West End YMCA. Cumming's reputation rested on a formidable finishing kick, but he had the disadvantage of having never before run a race as long as 15 miles. In any case, the chance to dazzle Longboat with his finishing kick didn't materialize because poor Cumming keeled over unconscious at the halfway point in the race. With Cumming gone, nobody else tested Longboat, and he trotted home the winner by a huge margin of 500 yards.

Next up for Longboat on Harry Rosenthal's schedule was an annual race held in Hamilton on an unlikely occasion – Christmas Day. The weather turned out to be happily snow-free but cold, and the race was over a course booby-trapped with icy patches. Once again, Bill Cumming emerged as Longboat's number one opponent, and this time, Cumming's finishing kick might come into play because the race covered only ten miles.

The event settled into a Longboat-Cumming duel, the two men comfortably neck and neck in front of everybody else. Then, just over seven miles into the race, a gang of thuggish spectators deliberately sent an empty buggy flying at the two runners. The thugs were backers of another runner, Joe Charles, who happened to come from the Six Nations too; they hoped that, by taking Longboat and Cumming out of commission, their man Charles would waltz to victory, and they would clean up in the betting. The buggy knocked Longboat and Cumming to the ground, but both scrambled up and took off in a rush that was fueled by their fright at the brush with disaster.

Neither man let up, still neck and neck, until the end of the race was in sight. Cumming reached for his famous finishing kick. Longboat responded with a kick of his own, and he won the kicking contest. Longboat finished first in a time of a little over 54 minutes, which broke the previous record for the Christmas Day Race by more than two whole minutes.

This string of early victories didn't seem to go to Longboat's head; he remained the same modest, easygoing fellow he had always been. But the wins may have affected Harry Rosenthal's sense of judgment because he entered Longboat in a race on February 11, 1907 that he didn't appear to stand a chance of winning. All the elements were stacked against Longboat. The race was indoors; Longboat had never, in his short career, run indoors. The distance was three miles; Longboat had so far established that he was stronger at much longer distances. And Longboat's sole opponent in the race was an American named George Bonhag, who happened to be an indoor ace and held many U.S. records – including the one for three miles.

The event took place as a special feature in a large track meet before 8,000 fans at the 74th Regiment Armory in Buffalo, New York: Bonhag's home turf. As soon as the race began, Longboat realized that he was in even more trouble than he had anticipated. His shoes were all wrong. He wore rubber-soled lacrosse shoes, which made him slip and slide on the wooden track. The much more experienced Bonhag, in his indoor spiked shoes, had no trouble holding the track's surface.

And Harry Rosenthal was hardly much help to Longboat. Rosenthal had brought along a pal from Toronto to assist with Longboat's coaching, but during the race, Rosenthal and the other man insisted on calling out contradictory advice.

"Run Bonhag off his feet, Tom!" Rosenthal shouted.

"Lay back, Tom!" the other man hollered.

Despite all the disadvantages, Longboat ran the race with extraordinary tenacity. The clever Bonhag held the inside position throughout the race, forcing Longboat to run on the outside and to cover more territory. And Longboat, in his slippery shoes, consistently lost ground on the corners. The size of the track, eight laps to the mile, meant that the runners turned through 96 corners. None of them was good news for Longboat.

Still, Bonhag could never shake his opponent. Longboat stuck to Bonhag's shoulder through virtually the entire race, and when the two men swung into the last lap, it was either runner's to win. In the end, at the last instant, Bonhag pulled a stride in front. He won by inches, but both men broke Bonhag's existing record for three miles. Longboat staggered off the track and was sick to his stomach in the exhaustion of his gallant effort.

"It was Tom's greatest race," Harry Rosenthal said that night – an opinion he kept repeating as long as he lived. "Tom lost, but the race against Bonhag was the greatest he ever ran."

Other men later took up Rosenthal's view – men who hadn't been near the 74th Armory on the night of the race – and whether it was accurate or not, it became a permanent part of Longboat lore that he never performed at such a high level of speed and courage as he did during the Bonhag race in Buffalo. But even if this remained the opinion of some racing experts of the period, it was also true that at the time of the Bonhag three-miler in February 1907, another race that would ultimately be remembered as Longboat's most famous, as opposed to possibly his greatest, was still two months away.

CHAPTER FOUR

Boston

The ancient story goes that when the Persians invaded Greece in 490 B.C., landing near the coastal village of Marathon, they outnumbered the Greeks by six to one and seemed certain to win the battle. But the ferocious defenders slaughtered 6,400 of the Persian enemy and sent the rest fleeing in their ships. A Greek messenger named Pheidippides, so the story continues, was despatched to Athens to deliver the glad news of the unexpected victory. Pheidippides raced the 24 miles from Marathon to Athens, pausing for nothing – not for rest nor water nor a change of sandals. He rushed to the ruling chamber in Athens, looked into the worried faces of the elders, and summoned the breath to shout: "Rejoice! We conquer!" His duty done, Pheidippides dropped dead.

There may be one false detail in this amazing tale – the part about Pheidippides probably never happened. The most reliable historian alive at the time, the eminent Herodotus, didn't write a word about the alleged run. A professional courier named Pheidippides turned up elsewhere in Herodotus's writings: it was he who carried an SOS to Sparta when the Persian fleet landed, a gruelling run of 150 miles in an astonishing 48 hours. But this Pheidippides not only survived the journey, he also conveyed the return news that the Spartans were too occupied with the fete of Carnea to send aid to the Greeks.

A later historian, Plutarch, wrote of a messenger who ran to Athens with word of a military victory, then collapsed in death, but this unfortunate fellow's name was Eucles. A good guess might be that, in the mists of time, the two tales of running and bravery — one from Herodotus and the other from Plutarch — became confused and merged.

One man who believed the story of Pheidippides's epic run in its pure dropping-dead version was Michel Breal, who taught philology — the science of languages — at the Sorbonne in Paris in the late 19th century. It developed that Professor Breal's belief would count for much in the emergence of long-distance running as a worldwide spectator sport. This was because Breal, in love with the concept of the epic run from Marathon, had the ear of a much more prominent Frenchman by the name of Baron Pierre de Coubertin.

De Coubertin's overwhelming ambition was to revive in the modern world the Olympic Games of Ancient Greece. Other men had unsuccessfully pursued the same dream, but de Coubertin was more determined than those who failed. The Greek Olympics had lasted from 776 B.C. to 394 A.D., staged every four years in celebration of the male body in athletic performance. The competitors engaged one another in such timeless sports as running, jumping, javelin throwing, boxing, and wrestling and in such less enduring contests as chariot racing. Some athletes put aside costumes and competed in the nude, the better to display the male body, and animal sacrifices were a ritual part of the Games, apparently for good luck.

De Coubertin's intense lobbying among interested nations led to the presentation of the first modern Olympics in April 1896, held for symbolic and political purposes in Greece. The de Coubertin version of the Games dropped the nudity and the sacrifices, and included — as well as the traditional contests in running, jumping, and in exhibitions of strength — a strange hodgepodge of activities that were popular in the 19th century but later faded from the competitive list. Among these were blindman's bluff, cannon shooting, fire fighting, tug-of-war, and leapfrog. At the urging of Professor Breal, the de Coubertin Games also added the long-distance race, which came to be known as the marathon. (The lengthiest race at the ancient Games covered a mere three miles.)

Thirty countries bringing along 311 competitors took part in the 1896 Games, and 25 of the athletes entered the marathon, which would duplicate the 24 miles that Pheidippides almost certainly didn't run from Marathon to Athens.

Twenty-one of the 25 marathoners were Greeks, and home country pressure was heavy for them to produce a victory. On the one hand, the winner, if he was Greek, was promised everything from a ton of chocolates to a lifetime of shaves; on the other hand, the rumor went around that if a Greek runner didn't win, all 21 of the country's entrants would be executed. Fortunately, the first man across the finish line was Spiridon Louis, a 24-year-old goatherd from the Greek hills of Marousel.

This first Olympic marathon — in fact, it was the first marathon run under any auspices — made a deep and favorable impression on one participant in particular, Arthur Blake. Representing the United States, Blake didn't do well in the race, collapsing after 14 miles and never finishing. But he returned home to his local organization, the Boston Athletic Club, and heaped praise on the marathon, on the exhilarating difficulty of the distance, the challenge, the athletic spectacle.

The Boston Athletic Club (BAC) caught Blake's enthusiasm, and the following April 19, Patriots' Day 1897, under the BAC's sponsorship, 15 men lined up outside Metcalf's Mill in the town of Ashland, Massachusetts, and ran the 24.5 miles to the Irvington Street oval in downtown Boston. The race was billed as the Boston Marathon. It wasn't the first race called a marathon ever run in the United States; there had been one a few months earlier in New York City. (A New Yorker named John McDermott won there and finished first again in Boston.) But it was the Boston race that generated lasting excitement among both runners and the sporting public. Distance running – anywhere from 5 to 20 miles – had caught on generally in North America and parts of Europe in the 1890s. Still, the Boston Marathon, the world's first annual race at the marathon distance, blossomed overnight into the sport's glory event.

There was no doubt that Tom Longboat was headed for the Boston Marathon's 1907 edition. But he was going without Harry Rosenthal. Rosenthal's slippery ways with expense money had landed both him and Longboat in hot water with the Amateur Athletic Union (AAU), the righteous body that had the responsibility of keeping the dreaded professionalism out of amateur sport in the United States. After Longboat's thrilling race against George Bonhag in Buffalo, the New York Athletic Club (NYAC) was keen to stage a rematch at its annual meet in Manhattan. Rosenthal demanded from the NYAC $150 in expense money. This sum was deemed so scandalously extravagant by the AAU, which figured Rosenthal must be pocketing much of the money as profit, that it and its Canadian counterpart suspended Longboat from further racing.

The suspension was soon lifted on the condition that Longboat get rid of Rosenthal as his manager. Longboat agreed, though he was unhappy about it since he genuinely liked Rosenthal. Then, in a move no doubt organized by Rosenthal, who never entirely disappeared from Longboat's life, Longboat joined the West End YMCA. The Y was a squeaky clean organization that easily satisfied the AAU. And the West End branch was a particular jewel in the Y's Toronto crown – its handsome three-story building at the southeast corner of Queen Street West and Dovercourt Road had been erected in 1889 in the style of a Victorian town hall, with a large gymnasium, an elegant assembly hall, and many smaller studios. Longboat took up training with the other Y runners (including his familiar rival, Bill Cumming), and in mid-April, he left for Boston chaperoned by the West End's director, a fussy man named Charles Ashley.

The fame that Longboat had gathered in previous months preceded him to Boston. "The Boston people took to the Indian as soon as we got there," Ashley later said. "They treated him like royalty." One Boston newspaper, frantic to get in on the whirl over Longboat but lacking a photograph of him, ran on its front page a picture of a Native football player, deliberately misidentifying him as Longboat. Any Native would do, it seemed, during the Tom love-in, as long as the Longboat name was attached to him.

The day of the race, Friday, April 19, came up unseasonably cold: 39°F (4°C), a raw wind, the nip of winter in the air. At noon, when the starting gun sent 126 runners away from Ashland, Longboat wore a sweater over his jersey to keep off the chill. He was content in the jostle of the first three miles to lay a couple of hundred yards off the pack of runners who sprinted to the front. Then, feeling warmer, preparing to increase his pace, he took off his sweater and tossed it to Ashley, who was accompanying Longboat in a slowly moving car. Ashley missed the toss, and the sweater fell into the road. Longboat turned back to retrieve it.

"No, no, Tom!" a panicky Ashley shouted. "Keep going!"

It was Longboat's favorite sweater. He wasn't going to risk losing it. He picked it off the road and dropped it in Ashley's lap. Behind Longboat, a dozen runners pounded past. Ashley moaned. Longboat grinned. He'd catch those guys – nothing to worry about. On the day of this Boston Marathon, Longboat was a man of impulsive confidence.

Confident Tom took the race's lead during its ninth mile. But not alone; he was running in tandem with two other competitors who gave the impression they were in it for the long haul. Sam Mellor was one of the front-running trio, a veteran racer from New York City and the 1902 Boston winner. And the other was an 18-year-old of absolutely no reputation named Charlie Petch from Toronto's North End Athletic Club.

Mellor was the first to fall out of the three-way battle, through no fault of his own. The Massachusetts police estimated the crowd along the race's route at 200,000 people, and just past the 12-mile mark, one of the 200,000 carelessly got his bicycle tangled with Mellor's legs. Mellor tumbled hard to the pavement. Charlie Petch seized the moment to speed away. Longboat stuck with Petch. Mellor, in pain, picked himself up and chased the other two. He caught them after a mile, but the effort tore the energy from his aching body, and very soon, he dropped far off the pace.

Through the next four miles, Longboat and the unheralded Petch kept up a two-runner duel for the lead. Neither man got an edge until, at 17 miles, they reached Newton Hills — two steep up-and-down slopes. Petch slipped into low gear. Longboat reached for high. He began steadily to put yards between himself and Petch — 50 yards, 100 yards, 200.

Walter Jeffreys, Petch's coach on a bicycle nearby, searched for words to encourage his runner. "Just a mile and a half to go, Charlie!" he shouted. It was a strategic lie. "Stay with it!"

A spectator spoiled Jeffreys's ploy.

"Don't believe it, lad!" the spectator called out. "It's seven miles that's left!"

Charlie Petch's shoulders sagged.

"I thought I was going to give the Indian the go-by at those hills," Petch explained later. "Then I felt numbed all of a sudden, and before I pulled myself together, he was gone."

Longboat was gone from Petch (who eventually finished sixth), gone from every runner on the course. No competitor was within three-quarters of a mile of Longboat at the race's end. He was all alone with the adoring multitude.

"Longboat," Charles Ashley later declared, "had to run through a crowd that wanted to reach out and hold him back from winning because they loved him! Yes, it was love!"

Longboat finished in a time of 2:24:25, which was an astonishing five minutes faster than the previous record (set in 1901 by Hamilton's Jack

Caffery). The governor of Massachusetts presented Longboat with a three-foot-high statue of Mercury, messenger to the Roman gods, and everybody cheered some more.

What was Longboat's response to the acclaim and affection?

"I want my supper," he said. "And I want it now."

The man had just run 25 miles. He was hungry. He ordered the chicken broth and a big steak.

Back in jubilant Toronto, the city council's Committee on Legislation and Reception met on Saturday, the day after the marathon, to plan civic honors for Longboat. The committee's decision, later approved by the full city council, was that there would be a parade, a reception at city hall, a gold medal, and – something unprecedented – a special $500 fund that, in words from the minutes of the committee meeting, would give Longboat "who is still a young man, an education to enable him to take a position in life." Little did city council or Longboat or Longboat's heirs dream that bureaucratic dithering would keep the money out of Longboat family hands until a much later Toronto mayor was in office: John Sewell in 1980.

A frenzy of celebration greeted Longboat when he stepped off the train from Boston the following Tuesday evening. Tens of thousands of people thronged the streets for the big parade; hundreds more hung from office windows. Three military bands blasted brassy tunes. There were firecrackers, skyrockets, blazing torches held high. Young men from eleven Toronto athletic organizations pranced and hurrahed. The lads of the West End Y chanted over and over the nonsense lines of the club's cheer:

> *Cannibal, cannibal*
> *Bowlegged bah*
> *West End, West End*
> *Rah, rah, rah!*

Toronto Reference Library

🥾 Toronto staged one of the greatest parades in its history to welcome Longboat after his victory in the 1907 Boston Marathon. This drawing, printed in the *Toronto Daily Star* on the day after the parade, presents an idealized version of Longboat at the grand reception.

And in the place of honor at the end of the parade, perched in the back-seat of an open car, draped in a large Canadian ensign, Longboat smiled shyly at the delirious Torontonians.

At city hall, Mayor Emerson Coatsworth and the other dignitaries escorted Longboat to the railing on the second floor, which overlooked the first floor rotunda, broad flights of stairs on either side. Rotunda and stairs were jammed with excited citizens. The mayor spoke words of greeting and praise. Then all eyes turned to Longboat.

"I thank you kindly, Mr. Mayor," Tom began confidently.

Longboat looked down at all the faces gazing up at him. Expectant faces, happy faces, but strange faces to Longboat. Strange white faces. Longboat froze. He couldn't find another word. Silence stretched through long, excruciating seconds. A whole minute.

"Speak up, Tom!" someone shouted from below.

Mayor Coatsworth stepped in front of Longboat and spoke briskly. "He says he thanks the people of Toronto for this great reception and hopes to be worthy of the honor done him."

Canada's Sports Hall of Fame

COG-WA-GEE
LONGBOAT

Longboat poses with the trophy he won for winning the 1907 Boston Marathon. Cog-wa-gee, which was Longboat's Onondaga name, translates as "Everything."

Everybody gave a lusty round of applause. The official party pushed through the crowd, piled into cars, and drove out to the West End Y. In the packed assembly hall, Charles Ashley held forth: "Longboat aspires to be the ideal man, not just perfect in body but in spirit and mind."

Longboat's boss from the Gage company, William Gundy, said in his speech that "Mr. Longboat is such a fleet-footed individual that we are thinking of putting him on the road." That drew plenty of chuckles.

Longboat grinned obediently through the long list of speakers, who didn't run out of wind until after midnight. Then he and a dozen West End friends went out to a late supper. But were they really friends?

Longboat had known the other Y runners for only a few weeks. Did they qualify as friends? Maybe not yet. Maybe he would never connect with these assured, preppy young white men. And there was no one he knew from the Six Nations at the supper, no pals from the reserve he had left just five months earlier. Longboat sat at the supper, the last event in a long night that paid tribute to his magnificent win in the Boston Marathon, and he felt more lonely than triumphant. More isolated than embraced.

CHAPTER FIVE

Triumph and Turmoil

harles Ashley reminded Longboat of his old teachers at the Mohawk
Institute in Brantford. Like the teachers, Ashley insisted on strict rules.
No alcohol for his runners, no dates with girls. But Longboat was a
social young guy whose late-adolescent hormones were galloping through
his system. He liked a glass of beer. He liked to step out with pretty young
ladies. Another thing about Ashley that annoyed Longboat was Ashley's habit
of booking Tom into races first and telling him about the bookings later. By
May 1907, in general disgust, Longboat quit the West End Y.

Almost immediately, he hooked up with an outfit called the Irish
Canadian Athletic Club (ICAC). There were many such clubs across Canada
– organizations that young Canadians joined to take part in track-and-field
events; some members enrolled as a means to get to the top level of competitive running, while others were in it simply for exercise and the pleasure of
athletic companionship.

The clubs were strictly male; few such organizations existed for women,
and it's a sign of how far female running lagged behind that women's track
wasn't included as an Olympic event until 1928. Women played a few other
sports in the early part of the 20th century: field hockey, skating, some ice
hockey, and a few water sports. But for the most part, participatory sports –
though they weren't nearly as popular as they have become today – were

mainly a male pursuit, with the emphasis on sports that didn't need a big layout in money for equipment. Lacrosse fit into that category as well as hockey, baseball, and snowshoeing.

Longboat's move to the Irish Canadian Athletic Club brought him under the influence of two men who would have a profound effect on his running career and on the ways in which he was perceived by racing fans of the period and by history books of the future. The first man was Tom Flanagan, a Toronto hotel owner and sports entrepreneur, and the second was Lou Marsh, a sportswriter for the *Toronto Daily Star*.

Flanagan, ten years older than Longboat, was a natty dresser and much given to talking the smooth, flattering, deceiving blarney that suited a man in the hospitality business. He and a partner, Timothy O'Rourke, owned the Grand Central Hotel at 57 Simcoe Street near the corner of Wellington in downtown Toronto. The saloon in the Grand Central was a hangout for a class of Torontonians who called themselves sportsmen. They were lawyers, stockbrokers, businessmen. They indulged in drinking and in the telling of tall tales. They adored sports, and even though some of them may not have played many games in their own youths, all considered themselves more knowledgeable and expert about sports than the athletes who performed in the competitions. They backed their opinions with money. Sportsmen loved to bet on sports events. And they loved their own image of themselves – champions, so they bragged, of fair play and sportsmanship.

Tom Flanagan was the ultimate sportsman, involving himself in sports even more deeply than the men who patronized the Grand Central. He gambled more lavishly than the others, and he took managerial roles in the careers of many of the athletes he backed with his money. For one significant period, he had a hand in lining up fights for Jack Johnson – the first black heavyweight boxing champion of the world – and served as a second in Johnson's corner for his historic knockout of the former champion, James J. Jefferies, in Reno, Nevada on July 4, 1910. But Flanagan's most ambitious venture into sports management was his founding of Toronto's Irish

Canada's Sports Hall of Fame

🥾 In the spring of 1907, Longboat (second from right) joined Toronto's Irish Canadian Athletic Club. Among his teammates was James Duffy (far left), who later won the 1914 Boston Marathon.

Canadian Athletic Club, for which he recruited many of the best young track-and-field athletes in eastern Canada. As of May 1907, by far the most prominent of the ICAC runners was Tom Longboat, the man whom Flanagan saw as his ticket to the world of big-time track and to the financial gain that went with it.

The second of the two men who shaped Longboat's career and legacy, Lou Marsh (no relation to John Marsh, the Winnipeg runner), joined the *Toronto Daily Star* as a 14-year-old copyboy in 1893. Within ten years, he was the *Star*'s number one sportswriter – a position he held, as both reporter and editor, until his death in 1936. In his young manhood, Marsh was a fine athlete. He played football for the Toronto Argonauts, and in track, he specialized in the sprints. When his playing days faded, he turned to officiating. He refereed hundreds of boxing matches all over Ontario and had a long career as a referee in the National Hockey League. The dual and simultaneous role of reporter and official wasn't unique to Marsh – Mike Rodden, a *Globe* sportswriter and editor, was another NHL referee – but it raised the possibility of conflicts of interest in the cozy community of early 20th-century North American sports.

Canada's Sports Hall of Fame

🏃 In this 1907 publicity photograph issued by Toronto's Irish Canadian Athletic Club, which Longboat had just joined, his home address is shown as 1186 Queen Street West, the boarding house where he lived when he was a member of the West End YMCA. In the group photo at the bottom, Longboat is seventh from the left.

Marsh had his first encounter of any length with Longboat when the two rode together on the train bringing Longboat back to Toronto from his marathon victory in Boston. "The man who says this Indian boy is not keen of wit knows not what he speaks of," Marsh wrote at the time. "His head is full of ideas and he is one of the great 'kidders' who ever came down the line to fame." The view of Longboat as a thoughtful, lively conversationalist was not one that Marsh stuck to for long. He changed his mind about Longboat early on, and the opinion he more frequently expressed in print was summed up in a story Marsh wrote toward the end of the runner's career: "In my time, I've interviewed everything from a circus lion to an Eskimo chief, but when it comes to being the original dummy, Tom Longboat is it. Interviewing a Chinese Joss or a mooley cow is pie compared to the task of digging anything out of Heap Big Chief T. Longboat."

Marsh's consistent characterization of Longboat as hopelessly monosyllabic and correspondingly stupid — an assessment that was accepted and repeated by later writers — derived in part from racism. Like many sports reporters of the time, Marsh seemed to view nonwhite athletes as a lesser species. They were splendid performers at their sports, perhaps, but not the white man's equal in moral and intellectual terms. Marsh wrote of blacks and Indians in stereotypes: Sam Langford, the great black boxer, was a "pickaninny," and Tom Longboat was "an Indian who could not be relied upon." But in the case of Longboat, a second motive might also have been at work in Marsh's writing: envy.

As a sprinter, Marsh ran under the colors of his very close friend Tom Flanagan. Marsh was a member of the Irish Canadian Athletic Club and therefore a Longboat teammate. On at least a couple of occasions, he was, in addition, a Longboat rival. At a track meet before 8,000 fans at the Ottawa Carnival on July 29, 1907, the feature event matched Longboat against a relay team of three other ICAC runners over five miles. The first two runners, experienced distance men named Hilton Green and Tom Coley, ran somewhat over two miles each, and the third runner covered the rest of the five miles. The third runner was Lou Marsh.

Coley finished the second leg against Longboat neck and neck, which meant Marsh set off on the final leg even with Longboat. Marsh, a speedy sprinter, opened up a quick and substantial lead. Longboat, now running his fifth mile of the race, began to whittle away at the gap between the two men. "Five feet from the tape," an unsigned report of the race in the *Star* said next day, "the white man was leading by six inches." Marsh may well have been experiencing flashes of triumph, nothing less than a victory over the mighty Longboat. "But at the finishing tape," the *Star* story continued, "the Indian, with a leap like a kangaroo, poked across just in front." Longboat won (and broke the Canadian record for five miles previously held by one of his opponents in the relay, Tom Coley).

Was the disappointment of Marsh's personal defeat enough to sour Marsh on Longboat? Probably not all by itself. But it – and a loss for Marsh in a similar relay featuring five runners against Longboat over four miles at the Toronto Police Games on August 22, 1907 – arguably contributed to the feelings of disdain for Longboat that Marsh began to express in his writing.

The Ottawa and Toronto relays were just two events in a busy schedule that Tom Flanagan laid out for Longboat in the 1907 track season. Flanagan entered Longboat in scores of races, driving him by car to those nearby, travelling by train to track meets in more distant places. In a five-mile match race at the Hanlan's Point Stadium on July 18, Longboat beat the powerful Irish-American runner J. J. Daley so thoroughly that the discouraged Daley detoured off the track just past the three-mile mark and headed straight to the dressing room.

In Hamilton on September 7, at a meet staged by the Irish Canadian Athletic Club of that city, Longboat took on John Marsh, his old Around the Bay rival, in a much anticipated five-mile race; but Longboat was overpowering on this day and forced Marsh, trailing by 300 yards at the time, to quit a half mile from the finish line. And in the annual Ward Marathon in

Canada's Sports Hall of Fame

🥾 In 1907, Longboat won races all over eastern Canada and the United States, including this Montreal race in November, when he cruised easily to victory.

October, lengthened to 20 miles in 1907, Longboat nonchalantly defeated a large field that included most of Canada's best distance runners.

These races and others proved profitable to Flanagan. He personally organized many of the meets at which Longboat was the drawing card, pulling in paying spectators by the thousands. Flanagan pocketed a big chunk of the proceeds, tapped into the expense money, and cleaned up by betting on Longboat. Tom was entirely Flanagan's creature at this stage of his career, supported and financed by Flanagan since Longboat, as an amateur, could accept no money from his many racing victories. He lived in a room at the Grand Central Hotel, and ate and drank there. Flanagan had no objection to a beer or two for his ICAC athletes. "Beer will stand by a man," he said, "and keep him from getting stale." Like the others in the ICAC, Longboat hoisted a glass at the Grand Central, where Flanagan took great delight in parading the champion runner for the benefit of his sportsmen cronies.

Flanagan treated the ever-obliging Longboat as his house pet in ways that now seem patronizing and offensive. He once made a bet with a pal named Barney O'Rourke of Caledonia that Longboat, on foot, could beat O'Rourke in his horse-drawn buggy from Hagersville to Caledonia – a distance of 18

Canada's Sports Hall of Fame

 In the fall of 1907, Longboat rode to city hall with three other famed Toronto athletes, all rowers. From left to right in the backseat are the legendary Ned Hanlan, Durnan, and Scholes. Longboat is seated beside the driver.

miles. O'Rourke's horse was sleek and strong (unlike the aged nag that Longboat outran a couple of years earlier in the fun race against his relative). And O'Rourke was so confident of victory that he casually waved Longboat to a head start while he made adjustments to his horse's harness and other gear. O'Rourke and the horse never made up the head start, and Longboat won the race to Caledonia. That gave Flanagan another humorous tale to spin for the entertainment of the sportsmen crowd at the Grand Central.

The one danger that Flanagan was nervous about in the way he was handling Longboat's career was that he could run into the same trouble that Longboat's first manager, Harry Rosenthal, encountered with the Amateur Athletic Union in the U.S. and its counterpart in Canada. The governing bodies might declare Longboat a professional and bar him from amateur competition. Flanagan intended to turn Longboat pro eventually, but not until the summer of 1908, after the Olympic Games, which were open only to competitors in good amateur standing. A victory in the Olympic marathon would put the final gloss on Longboat's running résumé and make him even more marketable on the growing professional racing circuit.

Flanagan needed to find a credible source of income for Longboat, something to project a public impression that Longboat, who had left employment at the Gage company, was paying his own way at the Grand Central. Flanagan hit on the idea of a cigar store. He took over the lease of a small establishment at 167 King Street West from a woman named Mrs. M. E. Oliver, who sold candy and other sweets on the premises. Flanagan remodelled the place and named it Tom Longboat Cigars. The store's location was promising since it was in the same building as the Princess Theatre, one of Toronto's leading centers for plays and musical entertainments. And because the store was also just a short stroll from the Grand Central, Flanagan could count on the sportsmen to drop by for their daily ration of cigars. All Longboat had to do, when he wasn't competing in races or training for them, was stand behind the counter and shake the customers' hands. That, Flanagan hoped, got around the professionalism problem.

Flanagan organized a pitch for Longboat at another source of cash. He went after the fund that Toronto City Council had voted for Longboat's education after his win in the Boston Marathon: $500 from the city plus an additional $250 contributed to the fund in small donations by generous Toronto citizens. The total, $750, represented a substantial sum in 1907, a time when a Toronto schoolteacher's annual salary amounted to $200, when a loaf of bread cost three cents, when newspapers sold for a penny a copy. The money, Flanagan reasoned, would tide Longboat over until he joined the professional circuit.

A letter dated November 29, 1907, over Longboat's signature, was delivered to R.T. Coady, treasurer of the city of Toronto. Almost certainly, the signature was Longboat's only contribution to the letter. The letter was perfectly typed; Longboat had no typing skills. And it was written in language and legal concepts that were beyond the sophistication of a 20-year-old with a grade four education. (The letter also bore a misaddress, coming from "165 King Street West," which was the address for the Ontario Society of Artists, next door to Tom Longboat Cigars.) The letter read:

165 King Street West,
Toronto, Nov. 29th, 1907.

R. T. Coady, Esq.,
City Treasurer.

Dear Sir:

      I understand you have collected a fund for my education. I do not want to accept it that way, as I am in business now and am getting enough education every day, and I am daily trying to improve myself in every way.

      Could you request the city to pay this money over to build a house for my mother on the Onondaga Reserve. The money could be spent by the Trustees, my mother to have the house for life and after her death it to go to me. I am told legislation will have to be obtained to sanction this.

      Have to thank who so kindly contributed, and the citizens of Toronto generally for helping me in every way while here.

      Kindly do what you can for me as above, and oblige,

      Yours truly,

Thomas Longboat

🥾 Longboat's manager, Tom Flanagan, wrote this letter for Longboat in an effort to coax from the city of Toronto the money it had set aside in a fund for Longboat's education after his victory in the 1907 Boston Marathon. The city held on to the money until 1980.

Toronto City Council debated the letter's request in several meetings; city lawyers pondered the legal points; city bureaucrats advised on policy. The sticking point was the word "education." Longboat's education "to enable him to take a position in life" was the purpose of the original resolution passed by city council. The building of a house for Longboat's mother (if this was to be the real use of the money and not just a scheme cooked up by Flanagan) didn't qualify as education, and the politicians couldn't figure a way around the problem. After years of stalling, council decided it was permissible to parcel out to Longboat the money donated to the fund by private Torontonians, though even this cautious step was taken grudgingly. Longboat received $50 in 1910, another $165 in 1911, and the final $35 in 1912. As for the $500 awarded by city council itself, the money remained in the city's bank account for the next seven decades.

Despite Flanagan's canniest manipulations, he couldn't avoid the wrath of the AAU in the U.S., which kept a sharp eye on Longboat's career and didn't like what it saw. Before the end of 1907, the AAU declared Longboat unwelcome in races under its jurisdiction. "Longboat will never run as an amateur in the United States," AAU President James Sullivan told the New York newspapers. "He has been a professional from the time he began his athletic career. He is taken from town to town by [Tom Flanagan] with bands and carriages and silk hats. He runs all kinds of races at country fairs for money."

The AAU ruling had many negative consequences for Longboat, meaning, among other things, that he was prevented from defending his Boston Marathon championship in April 1908. But, as far as Flanagan was concerned, the news was not all bad. The Canadian AAU refused to go along with the American body's ban on Longboat. This decision kept Longboat's amateur career alive and active in Canada, and most significantly, it put him on schedule to compete in the Olympic Games. Canadian track officials counted on Longboat to bring home the marathon championship. So did excited Canadian sports fans. So did money-hungry Tom Flanagan. And so did the man himself — the best of all distance runners — Tom Longboat.

CHAPTER SIX

Tom's Great Olympic Misadventure

Long-distance running enthralled the family of King Edward VII and Queen Alexandra of England as much as it did the rest of the racing fans among their loyal subjects. So when London played host to the fifth Olympic Games in the last two weeks of July 1908, their majesties asked that the marathon event begin from a spot where royal family members could watch. This would be on the grounds of their castle at Windsor. The marathon's starting line was originally set in the middle of the town of Windsor; from there, the route for the race wound east along roads and byways to the huge stadium at Shepherd's Bush in London. But Olympic officials bowed to their majesties' wishes and pulled the starting line back to a point close to the royal apartments in Windsor Castle. It was a decision that stretched the race by several hundred yards.

Until then, the marathon's length had varied dramatically at different venues: 24 miles at the first Olympics, closer to 25 in Boston, more than that in other marathons. The distance from Windsor Castle to Shepherd's Bush added up to 26 miles, 385 yards, and for some reason – most likely as a practical matter of at last regularizing the marathon – this became the standard distance for all marathons in the future, adopted by racing bodies throughout the world.

🥾 In the week before the Olympic Games in London, England at the end of July 1908, the Canadian team took a day off for relaxation.

Opposite, Longboat is standing at the rear.

Longboat is seated at the front of the boat, with his legs dangling over the bow.

Longboat is standing at the far right.

Tom Longboat was the pre-race favorite to win the now regularized Olympic marathon. He went to the Games as a member of Canada's first-ever government-supported Olympic team. Canadian athletes had competed in earlier Games on their own, covering expenses out of personal funds, and not as members of a team. The début 1908 team included 24 track-and-field athletes under head coach Bill Sherring, the marathon winner at the 1906 Intercalated Olympics, and of the 24, no fewer than 13 were entered in the marathon. A couple of weeks in advance of the Games, Sherring escorted his team to London, where they took up residence in the Sussex Hotel and went into final training. Conspicuous by his absence from the Sussex was Longboat. The reason was that Tom Flanagan insisted that Longboat, his personal charge, needed special treatment.

In early June, Flanagan took Longboat to the old Flanagan homestead in the town of Kilmallock in Ireland's county Limerick. Part of Flanagan's motive was to show off Longboat, whose fame had spread around the world, to Flanagan's Irish friends and relatives. The rest of his motive was to allow Longboat to sharpen his conditioning for the Olympics. Both objectives appeared to be realized.

According to reports from a press service journalist, Longboat made two exhibition runs through the Limerick countryside – one of 13 miles, the other of 20. Dozens of policemen were needed for both events to clear the roads of the thousands of spectators who arrived from all over Ireland to watch the Onondaga runner they'd heard so much about. As for conditioning, Flanagan told the journalist, "Longboat is in the shape of his life." But much later, as we shall see, Flanagan changed his tune about the effectiveness of Longboat's training in Limerick.

Ten days before the marathon, Flanagan moved Longboat to London. But he didn't hand Tom over to Bill Sherring for conditioning purposes, as would be expected. Instead, he put Longboat under the care of none other than Lou Marsh, who was in London to cover the Games for the *Toronto Daily Star*. Marsh assumed training responsibilities for Longboat, though he and Flanagan kept this assignment a secret, and without mentioning his dual role, Marsh reported to *Star* readers that "Longboat looks fit to run the race of his life" and that "he is in perfect physical condition and sleeps like a baby." As with Flanagan, however, Marsh later had a different story to tell about Longboat and his dedication to training in London.

As part of his Longboat duties, Marsh checked out the new macadam surface that covered much of the marathon's route. "Hard as flint," he concluded. Jack Caffery agreed. Caffery, the Hamilton runner who had won two Boston Marathons and was a member of the '08 Olympic team, took a practice run over the course. "Every man will wear out a pair of shoes on the journey," he said afterwards. "I just finished wearing out mine."

(The additional point that Caffery's remarks made was that manufacturers of running shoes hadn't yet developed a shoe that adequately withstood the pounding of a marathon. Distance runners had two basic styles to choose from: either heavy leather boots resembling the kind that soldiers wore, or low-cut shoes with leather uppers and soles. Neither shoe had much flexibility, and both were often painful to run in. What added to the pain problem was that most runners chose to wear no socks, a fact that combined with the stiffness of the leather to make blisters a frequent difficulty. It wasn't until a few years later that shoe manufacturers discovered the rubber technology to create shoes that offered marathoners more comfort and durability.)

The marathon route from Windsor to Shepherd's Bush presented other problems. It lay along a series of twisty roads, with many sharp turns and with some passages so narrow that two competitors couldn't run through them side by side. None of this looked promising for any marathoner. Nor did the weather on the day of the race – Friday, July 24 – offer much relief. Heavy rain had fallen earlier in the week, but marathon day turned up punishing in its heat and humidity.

In these conditions, 58 runners gathered in the early afternoon of the appointed day on the grounds of Windsor Castle. The small audience consisted almost entirely of royal family members plus a handful of Olympic officials. Two kings-to-be were among the children – the future Edward VIII and George VI. Both had new cameras that they aimed at the politely posing marathoners.

For the comfort of the older royals, the starting line was ringed with scarlet upholstered gilt chairs and a round table on which rested a large bowl of red roses. The table also held an electric button, and at 2:33 P.M., the future kings' mother and a future queen herself – Mary, princess of Wales – pressed the button. It relayed a signal to the senior British Olympic official, Lord Desborough, who was sitting in a nearby automobile. Lord Desborough leaned out the car window and fired two shots in the air from his starter's pistol. The Olympic marathon was underway.

As the gentle clapping of the royals faded in the background, the runners trotted through the hush of the vast lawns of Windsor Castle. Outside the grounds, a large contingent of schoolboys from nearby Eton College swelled the waiting crowd, and when the runners burst through Windsor's gates, the Etonians' falsetto cheers shattered the silence.

Longboat was among the leaders at the gates, and he stayed there, not less than 100 yards off the front runners through the first five miles. At that point, five miles out, Lou Marsh, on a bicycle, pulled alongside Longboat. Marsh was present in his two capacities – one open and the other secret – as a *Toronto Daily Star* reporter and as Longboat's unofficial minder.

Marsh had a bicycling companion – a Toronto man named Doc Morton, who was a bike racer. From time to time during the next dozen miles, Morton sped ahead to look over the runners among the leading pack.

"They're running as if the devil himself were behind them!" he reported back to Marsh after one reconnaissance trip.

Marsh liked the sound of that. He had a theory that the other runners were driven by fear of Longboat; they thought, in Marsh's view, that they needed to build a lead sufficient to hold off Longboat in the race's finishing stretch. But Marsh was certain such a strategy played into Longboat's hands, that he had the stamina to overhaul the others, who would tire from the frantic early pace.

By the 17-mile mark, the race seemed to have settled into a contest among a few serious contenders. One was Longboat. Two others had Canadian connections, though they weren't running for Canada. Charles Hefferon was one of the two, a man who grew up on the Canadian Prairies but represented the country of his new citizenship, South Africa; the other was John Hayes, an American who spent his youth in the Ottawa area. A fourth potential winner was Dorando Pietri of Italy. He was a baker from Capri, a colorful and game little man, unmistakable in his vivid red racing shorts, a competitor who had become so popular that he was identified by just one name − Dorando − in the same way that, today, sports fans know they don't need to attach a last name to the golfer Tiger Woods.

Going into mile 20, Hefferon held the lead by about 300 yards over Longboat, who had out-duelled Dorando for second place, while Hayes lurked further back. And that was the order of the runners when Longboat's race fell apart.

He had just entered a stretch of roadway that was treeless and open to the sun's fierce glare. Despite the harsh conditions, he appeared to be running with confidence. In not much more than the blink of an eye, all of that changed. Longboat suddenly thrust his arms in the air and staggered one or two paces. His body quivering violently, he tumbled toward the ground. He bounced off a wheel on Marsh's bicycle, then rolled into the road. He was, Marsh later said, "senseless."

Marsh and Morton jumped off their bikes and scrambled to the fallen Longboat. Marsh was carrying a flask of champagne for use as a stimulant. He poured some into the unconscious Longboat's mouth. Longboat began to stir just as an Olympic medical officer arrived on the scene.

"This man is dead beat," the medical officer said of Longboat. It wasn't much of a technical diagnosis, but the official's next words spelled the end

Toronto Star

Lou Marsh was a man of simultaneous and conflicting roles: a sportswriter and editor for the *Toronto Daily Star* for forty-three years, an NHL referee (as shown above), Longboat's secret trainer, and a writer who frequently mistreated Longboat in print.

of Longboat's Olympics. "I won't let him go on," the medical man announced. Longboat, weak and shaky, was guided into an automobile for transport to the Shepherd's Bush Stadium.

With their man out of the race, Marsh and Morton climbed back on their bikes to chase the other runners through the last miles. What they saw was a race that produced the most bizarre finish in the history of the Olympic marathon.

The plucky little Dorando passed Hefferon in the two miles leading up to Shepherd's Bush, and it was Dorando who entered the stadium first. But almost immediately, the 65,000 spectators realized that Dorando was struggling with disorientation. To complete the race, he needed only to turn left and run two-thirds of the way around the track to the finish line. In a mental fog, Dorando turned right. Several officials reached out and guided him in the correct direction. Dorando staggered for 50 yards and collapsed. Officials lifted him off the track and again shoved him on his way. Dorando collapsed twice more. Each time, friendly officials revived him, carried him a few yards, gave him pushes and small pats of comfort until Dorando at last tottered across the finish line.

Seconds after Dorando's questionable triumph, John Hayes entered the stadium. He, too, had passed Hefferon. Hayes finished second, then Hefferon, then another American named Joseph Forshaw. An Italian flag was run up over the stadium to mark Dorando's victory, and Queen Alexandra presented the woozy little runner with a gold cup. But the American Olympic delegation objected to the win on the very good grounds that Dorando had been illegally assisted to the finish line. Before the day was over, Olympic officials moved swiftly to uphold the American protest, to disqualify Dorando, to declare Hayes the Olympic champion, and to bump all the other finishers up one place in the final standings.

Meanwhile, Longboat, Flanagan, and Marsh were busy explaining why the pre-race favorite, Longboat, had flamed out. Flanagan contributed little of value to the discussion because he had passed the hours of the marathon sitting in the stadium where he expected to watch his man come home in first place. Marsh, still concealing his part in Longboat's training, never really addressed Longboat's collapse, but stuck to his theory that Longboat had possessed the stamina to whip the field. The trouble, in Marsh's opinion, lay with the course and its twisty nature. "If the race had been over a road with a straight stretch where Longboat could have seen the leader," Marsh insisted, "he would have won handily."

As for Longboat, he blamed the ferocious heat for his troubles. The sun and humidity had combined in the 20th mile to hit him with the suddenness and power of a heavyweight's punch. Three weeks later, Longboat added another factor. On Tuesday, August 3, when he and Flanagan sailed into New York City on board an ocean liner named the *Kronprinz Wilhelm*, Longboat told the waiting newspaper reporters that "the pounding on the hard pavement knocked me out."

An important gentleman named J. Howard Crocker had a more sinister explanation. Crocker was the manager of the Canadian Olympic Team, and in that capacity, he examined Longboat shortly after the fallen runner arrived at Shepherd's Bush. Crocker said he noted Longboat's "weak pulse" and "pinpoint pupils," and in a later document titled "Report of the First Canadian Olympic Athletic Team," Crocker reached this conclusion: "I think that any medical man knowing the facts of the case will assure you that the presence of a drug in an overdose was the cause of [Longboat's] failure."

It happened that the drug of choice among several distance runners of the time was strychnine. Taken in tiny doses, a fraction of an ounce (under five milligrams), strychnine acted as an energizing agent. In a slightly larger quantity, it caused the body to convulse painfully (not unlike the physical contortions that Longboat appeared to go through in the moment of his collapse). Slightly more strychnine produced paralysis of the respiratory system, resulting in death. As a demonstration of strychnine's lethal properties, its common use has always been as a poison for rats, and from time to time, it has been a murderer's favorite means of eliminating a victim. Nobody is certain precisely how and when strychnine came into practice as a racing stimulant, but it was apparently common enough in the early 20th century that one track historian could confidently write of the 1908 Olympic marathon: "Dorando Pietri had doped himself with strychnine, like most of the others in the race."

Likely it was the coaches and managers rather than the runners themselves who administered the strychnine. This could be done without the approval or knowledge of the runners since strychnine is colorless and odorless, though its bitter taste could be a giveaway in water, or in most other liquids. If Longboat had been slipped a dose of strychnine before the Olympic marathon, then only two men could have done the deed: Flanagan or Marsh. It's unlikely that Marsh would have acted on his own, and Flanagan could hardly have pulled off a drugging without Marsh catching on. The most logical supposition, if Longboat was given a shot of strychnine, was that Marsh, the trainer, handled the administering of the drug on the instructions of his friend, Flanagan, the manager.

In all his writings about the Olympics, Marsh never discussed the drugging possibility, but after J. Howard Crocker's damning report, Flanagan spoke about the issue. "Stimulants were resorted to," he said, "when Longboat was on the ground bleeding from nose and mouth. But no power on earth could have made Tom move in his helpless condition." The "stimulants" Flanagan referred to could only have been the champagne that Marsh poured into Longboat after the latter's collapse. The "bleeding" was almost certainly Flanagan's own exaggerated spin on Longboat's condition. No one else mentioned blood — not Marsh nor Crocker nor Longboat himself — only Flanagan, who was miles from the scene of Longboat's swoon.

Flanagan had something else on his mind that complicated the drug question. "If Longboat had not failed us in the English marathon and had won," Flanagan later explained, "I would have toured the world with him and he would have retired worth a quarter million. I had the financial backing and I had the tour all arranged." Such a tour would also have made a richer man of Flanagan, a prospect that perhaps opened up two possibilities: either Flanagan had strychnine administered to Longboat in an effort to guarantee an Olympic victory and the subsequent lucrative tour, or else Flanagan steered clear of the use of strychnine or any other stimulant out of fear of harming Longboat and jeopardizing the tour. If it was the former, then strychnine in an accidental overdose was probably to blame for Longboat's collapse; if the latter, then it was the heat, humidity, hard roads, and winding route that did him in. Since drug testing for athletes was unheard of in 1908, the question of Longboat's drugging – was he or wasn't he? – was never resolved.

Fourteen years after the London Olympics, Marsh and Flanagan produced yet another explanation for Longboat's failure in the big race. As we've seen, in the weeks before the ill-fated London marathon, Marsh and Flanagan had spread the word that Longboat, training diligently, was in the most splendid shape of his young career. But in an article that Marsh wrote in the December 2, 1922 *Star Weekly*, a magazine supplement published each week in the *Toronto Daily Star*, he and Flanagan presented a version of Longboat's pre-Olympic preparation habits that entirely contradicted the two men's 1908 statements about Longboat's condition.

The article itself amounted to a cruel attack on Longboat, portraying him at length as just another foolish and stubborn Indian. Specifically on the subject of the Olympic disaster, Marsh quoted Flanagan with this 1922 recollection of 1908: "[Longboat] wouldn't train. I couldn't handle him in Ireland, and the man I turned him over to in England ten days before the race had all he could do to keep track of him there." Marsh, admitting for the first time in print that he was "the man in England," picked up on Flanagan's theme of the elusive, disobedient Longboat and expanded on it. "[Longboat] was as hard to train as a leopard and harder to watch than a chunk of loose lightning." And, further: "You couldn't keep track of [Longboat] without handcuffs, leg irons, a straight jacket, and a regiment of Pinkertons." ("Pinkerton" was a name given to private detectives, members of Pinkerton's National Detective Agency.)

The blame for the Olympic flop, according to Marsh and Flanagan in their 1922 version of events, lay on the shoulders of Longboat alone, the hopeless Indian who refused to train and who, in Marsh's words, "did not have a white man's business brain." This wasn't the view that Marsh and Flanagan shared with the public back in 1908. Did they share it with Longboat at the time? It's impossible to say. What is certain is, whether or not Marsh and Flanagan criticized him in person, that Longboat didn't waste much time back in Canada after the Olympics in showing that the disappointment in London hadn't affected his winning ways in long-distance running.

CHAPTER SEVEN

A Professional among Professionals

I n a sense, Flanagan and Marsh were probably right about Longboat's slack training habits. But theirs was a judgment measured by the standards of competitive running in the accepted world of track and field. It was a white man's judgment – one that didn't take into account Longboat's racing roots. He came from a much different running background, from a tradition that was distinctly Native and that departed from white practices in many key areas.

For centuries, running was fundamental to life among all the Native nations of North America. Running figured into hunting, into the delivering of messages, and the trading of goods. Runners warned of attacks from outsiders and carried plans for a nation's own aggressions. The fastest and most durable runners were crucial members of their nations. "The runners," one historian wrote, "were communicators of culture. They were regarded as safekeepers of accurate information, and their units were absorbed into social and religious life."

It was the system of organized runners that enabled the Iroquois Confederacy to dominate Upper New York State in the long period before the Six Nations moved north. The 240-mile Iroquois Trail bound together the Confederacy from the eastern door of the Mohawk (near present-day Albany, New York) to the western door of the Seneca (just beyond Buffalo).

With rest periods, Iroquois runners covered the Trail in about 70 hours, carrying messages, solidifying the government, maintaining the links among the Confederacy's nations that kept them united.

Within the runners' own communities, they took part in regular races to entertain themselves, their friends, and neighbors. But the races were for pleasure, and their outcome didn't confer stardom on the winners. "Indian fans," the historian quoted above wrote, "did not project fantasies of athletic success on to public figures since nearly everybody ran." Running was much respected, but, in the familiar Native concept, winning a race was one among many undertakings, all treasured to the same degree: telling a story, paddling a canoe, preparing a meal.

It's probably an exaggeration to say that Longboat, coming at the end of the long line of runners in the Native nations, was in effect genetically programmed to run. And it isn't known whether he possessed the physical attributes that have been found in more recent years in the best marathoners: the slow pulse rate and the higher percentage of short twitch muscle fiber. But it's certain that he had the same gifts as the great Native messenger runners of the past. And he brought to racing similar attitudes of modesty and informality that his ancestors accepted as natural.

Training wasn't for Longboat the rigid business that Flanagan, Marsh, and the other white men preached. Longboat liked to play handball and take long hikes. That, he undoubtedly thought, was enough to keep himself in shape, and besides, he ran in so many races that he was rarely far from competitive physical condition. Even relaxing on his own over a few beers and sitting up nights with his friends struck him as normal. The latter conduct exasperated Flanagan, who thought Longboat went beyond even Flanagan's tolerant attitude to his athletes' drinking and socializing. But it was the less rigorous approach that, whether Longboat himself was aware of it or not, was part of the Native running heritage. Whatever Flanagan and the other whites said, Longboat was stubborn enough to handle running his own way.

Back from London in the summer of 1908 and returning to regular competition in Canada, Longboat's own way seemed to be working. His first post-Olympic race came on August 15 at a Saturday afternoon meet in Hamilton, Longboat in a three-mile match against Fred Simpson, a Mississauga Native from Peterborough, Ontario. Simpson was no pushover. He had finished sixth in the Olympic marathon – the highest placed Canadian. But in Hamilton, Longboat easily handled Simpson in a respectable time.

The following Wednesday, at the Police Games in Toronto, Longboat surprisingly lost a five-mile race to Percy Sellen, a clubmate at the Irish Canadian Athletic Club. Longboat had an excuse for the defeat: three hours before the race, he indulged himself in a meal of boiled beef, potatoes, and cabbage, and the weight of the heavy food slowed him down. Three days later, in a return match against Sellen in another five-miler at the Hamilton Jockey Club track, Longboat chose from a more sensible pre-race menu and won by a convincing margin.

Canada's Sports Hall of Fame

Longboat shows his form in outdistancing an unidentified opponent in a 1908 race at the Hanlan's Point Stadium on the Toronto Islands.

Canada's Sports Hall of Fame

👞 In the fall of 1908, before Longboat turned professional, he and the man who would become his fiercest rival, Alf Shrubb of England, size each other up near the Grand Central Hotel in downtown Toronto (corner of Wellington and Simcoe Streets), where both men were then living.

Other victories followed – a third straight win in the Ward Marathon, a first place in a five-mile race in Halifax in Canadian-record time, wins at shorter distances in Ontario county fair events.

By late autumn, Flanagan decided the time was ripe to turn Longboat professional. A New York City sports promoter named Pat Powers helped the decision by putting an offer on the table that Flanagan couldn't resist. The controversial finish in the Olympic marathon had given distance running an extra boost in popularity, and Powers intended to cash in by staging a series of indoor match races over the marathon distance at Madison Square Garden.

For the first race on November 25, Powers pitted the two major figures in the London controversy against one another: Italy's Dorando Pietri versus the U.S.'s John Hayes. Both enjoyed huge popularity in the New York area, Dorando because the city had a large Italian immigrant population and Hayes because he was a local fellow who worked at the well-known Bloomingdale's department store (which set up a track on the store's roof where Hayes could train). The race drew a sellout crowd and sent the Italian fans home happy when Dorando beat Hayes by 60 yards in a fast time. Now, Pat Powers said to Flanagan, Longboat was next: Longboat versus Dorando on December 15 at the Garden.

In early December, Longboat headed to New York to train for the big race. He was accompanied by Flanagan and a Flanagan entourage, and he had just arrived when he received a letter that threw him off his training. Earlier that year, he had met and courted a young woman named Lauretta Maracle. She was from the Mohawk reserve on the Bay of Quinte, 110 miles east of Toronto, and she became engaged to marry Longboat. A man from the Six Nations who had no use for Longboat wrote to Lauretta's brother, warning him that Longboat was "worthless" and that the brother should stop the planned marriage of Longboat and Lauretta. The brother, a Mohawk chief, forwarded the letter to Longboat, whose spirits sank. Flanagan came to the rescue by bringing Lauretta to New York, where the future bride swore to Longboat that she intended to be his wife forever. Reassured, Longboat resumed training.

At precisely nine o'clock on the night of the race, before a packed Garden, Dorando made a splashy entrance draped in a fur-lined overcoat. The large and delirious Italian contingent in the crowd showered him in flowers of welcome and gave Dorando a roaring cheer that made the building rattle. These fans had already pooled their money to buy a $500 diamond medal, which they planned to present to the night's winner. They had no doubt the recipient would be their beloved Dorando.

A few minutes later, Longboat arrived on the track to a much less fervent greeting. He had on white running shorts decorated in red and green rosettes, which Lauretta had sewn into the fabric. Longboat planned to wear his Irish Canadian Athletic Club jersey – the one with the green maple leaf and the Irish harp – but he'd left the jersey at home. Fortunately another ICAC member in New York had packed his own club jersey, and he lent it to Longboat, which explains why Longboat ran the race wearing Lou Marsh's shirt.

The race got under way at 9:14, and Dorando went straight to the front, a position he held for the majority of the 262 laps. Dorando, a full head shorter than Longboat, ran in a dogged, earnest style. Each time he came around the track, his trainers sprayed him with squirts from a row of seltzer bottles. This was intended to jar him into an even faster pace, but it meant that Dorando ran with soaked jersey and shorts plastered to his body. The trainers also fuelled Dorando from an assortment of beverages: wine, distilled water, and coffee heated on a small alcohol stove at the side of the track.

Longboat had a much longer stride than Dorando, and even though he seemed inexplicably off his best form on this night, his stride kept him close to the determined Dorando. Flanagan, Flanagan's brother Mike, and an ICAC trainer named Tom Eck acted as Longboat's seconds. They gave the runner occasional seltzer sprays, handed him cups of water and thimblefuls of champagne, and warned him not to let Dorando open up a significant lead. The fear in the Longboat camp was that a fast early pace by Dorando would put the subpar Longboat away for good, that he would never catch his opponent if he got a lap or more ahead.

But Dorando couldn't shake Longboat, and after 15 miles, the two men were taking turns holding brief leads. Past 20 miles, the pace was slowing, and at times, both runners moved at a rate not much faster than a brisk walk. In the 22nd mile, Flanagan pulled a small trick to give Longboat a psychological boost: he sent Lauretta onto the edge of the track, running alongside her fiancé for a few yards, waving encouragement.

Entering the 25th mile, Dorando showed painful signs of increased fatigue. He wobbled, and he shook. Longboat pushed in front. The two men persevered until six laps remained in the race. Dorando chased Longboat for two of the laps, but, ultimately, staggering in pursuit of his rival, he tumbled into a barrier at the side of the track and collapsed. The little runner hovered on the edge of unconsciousness. He was through for the night, but that didn't make Longboat the certain and official winner. He still had to finish the last four laps. He was fiendishly tired, but he kept his legs moving, like a man on automatic pilot, and at last, he crossed the finish line. Flanagan and his hotel partner, Tim O'Rourke, hoisted the weary Longboat on their shoulders for a small parade of victory in the first great race of Tom's professional career.

Longboat recovered enough to celebrate, and he and some of Flanagan's entourage went on the town until daybreak. But at some point, Longboat vanished. No one knew where he'd gone until he was tracked several hours later to the Seville Hotel. The Seville was where Dorando and his brother Ulpiano were staying in Manhattan, and Longboat was in Dorando's room offering comfort to his discouraged rival. It made for an odd encounter since Longboat spoke no Italian and Dorando's English was minimal. Still, Dorando appreciated Longboat's generous and thoughtful concern. He didn't even mind the $500 diamond medal that Longboat wore on his jacket.

In the following days at home in Toronto, Longboat and Lauretta prepared for their wedding, which was set for Monday, December 28. Lauretta was seven years older than Longboat, petite and pretty. "She is a winsome little girl," the *Globe* reported condescendingly, "who has, she says, been educated away from many of the traditions of her race. She does not talk of feathers, war paint or other Indian paraphernalia." Lauretta, who apparently had a will of iron, was a devout Anglican and insisted that Longboat join her church. On December 22, the two travelled to the town of Deseronto on Lauretta's Mohawk reserve, where the Reverend Alfred Creegan baptized Longboat into the Anglican faith. Longboat's friends suspected that he was taking the step more to please Lauretta than out of a deep religious conviction.

Canada's Sports Hall of Fame

Shortly before their wedding on December 28, 1908, Longboat and his bride-to-be, Lauretta, pose for a formal portrait.

👟 Longboat married his first wife, Lauretta Maracle, on December 28, 1908 in this charming Anglican church, St. John the Evangelist, on Portland Street in downtown Toronto. The church was torn down in 1963 shortly after this photograph was taken.

Six days later, Longboat, Lauretta, and the rest of a small wedding party gathered at St. John the Evangelist, a small Anglican church, simple and elegant in architectural style, at the corner of Portland and Stewart Streets, just west of Toronto's downtown business district. The party included none of Longboat's older friends, no family members, no one from the Six Nations. The men present were limited to those Longboat had met through running: his first manager, Harry Rosenthal, and the ICAC crowd including Tim O'Rourke, Lou Marsh, and Mike Flanagan. The best man was Tom Flanagan, who took his duties so casually that he forgot to bring the wedding licence that Longboat had entrusted to him. That delayed the ceremony 30 minutes while Flanagan went back to the Grand Central to fetch the licence before the Reverend Creegan could join the couple in holy matrimony.

It was Flanagan who orchestrated the wedding reception. For the occasion, he rented the city's most prestigious concert hall – Massey Hall – and extended an open invitation to Longboat's fans to attend the public event. More than 1,000 people showed up to watch a vaudeville show stage-managed by Flanagan and featuring an odd collection of entertainers: a female impersonator, a lady soprano, a boy monologist, a solo trumpeter, and Hedder & Son, comedy acrobats. The inevitable speeches followed, including one delivered by ICAC secretary D'Arcy Hinds that was partly in Gaelic, a language few others in the hall understood. As the event stretched into its third hour, Mr. and Mrs. Longboat at last took to center stage, where they stood for another hour shaking the hands of a long line of well-wishers. Finally Flanagan pronounced the reception a success, and everyone went home.

The Longboats had no time for a honeymoon because Flanagan had booked a 25-mile Longboat-Dorando rematch at the 74th Regiment Armories in Buffalo on the Saturday after the wedding. The race ended in anticlimax, with Dorando abruptly quitting in the 19th mile, but the contest still packed plenty of drama. Dorando began at a flying pace, far faster than in the New York race. In the second mile, as Longboat struggled to keep up, he slipped on the track, which was dangerously uneven – hard as concrete in some parts, spongy in others. Longboat caught a soft patch and crashed down on one knee. When he stood up, the knee was gashed and bleeding. Longboat's chances of winning seemed suddenly in peril.

But in a show of courage, Longboat forced himself to match Dorando's swift pace. Longboat's time for the first 15 miles was only eight seconds short of his own Canadian record at the distance, a remarkably fast clip for a 25-mile race. Still, Dorando held the lead for 16 of the first 18 miles, and he was ahead of Longboat in the 19th mile when he stunned the crowd – 11,000 screaming fans squeezed into a building intended for 8,000 – by unexpectedly veering off the track. Dorando was worn out and, worse for him, he was discouraged that his relentless show of speed had failed to take the resolve out of Longboat. Dorando put his hand over his heart and allowed his brother Ulpiano to guide him to the dressing rooms.

Longboat still had six miles to cover before he could claim the official win. His gashed knee was beginning to swell, and his feet – pounding on the track's odd mix of surfaces – were developing large, bleeding blisters. He slowed to a walk. Three men in civilian clothes appeared on the track to escort him round and round the oval. The three were Tim O'Rourke, Bill Sherring, and the ever-present Lou Marsh, who was in Buffalo to report the race for the *Star*. The men walked beside Longboat, and for the final mile, as a show for the fans, Longboat ignored his pain and stepped up to a slow and easy lope, with Sherring and Marsh still pacing him to the finish line.

With the win, Longboat seemed on top of the world. He was 21 years old, newly married, and famous as probably the best of all distance runners. He was making a good deal of money, and the prospects were for even more financial rewards since he had a deal to run another race at Madison Square Garden on January 26 against an English professional named Alf Shrubb, who would become Longboat's foremost rival over the following years. Everything was full of promise and prosperity for Longboat, but what he couldn't know on the night of his brave victory over Dorando was that a demoralizing shock was waiting for him the very next week.

CHAPTER EIGHT

Under New Management

Tom Flanagan had put his brother Mike in charge of Longboat's training in the autumn of 1908. The job involved rousing Longboat out of bed, organizing his breakfast (invariably an egg with a dash of sherry, porridge, toast, and tea), and accompanying him on two daily ten-mile walks – one in the morning and a second in the early evening. But 48 hours after the Dorando race, Mike Flanagan announced he was resigning.

"Longboat," Flanagan told the Toronto newspapers, "is the most contrary piece of furniture I ever had anything to do with."

Longboat was mildly upset at Mike's departure, but much more disturbing news came on January 11 when the other Flanagan, Tom, revealed that he was following his brother out the door. He had been Longboat's manager for most of two years, the best man at his wedding two weeks earlier, and now Flanagan was dropping the man who was his star runner and his supposed friend. He offered one explanation. "My business interests," Flanagan said, "demand the attention I could not give them and look after the Indian as closely as he must be looked after."

Lou Marsh suggested another reason for his pal's defection. According to Marsh, Flanagan was troubled by rumors that had persisted since the Olympics that he might have used drugs or other means to rig more than one Longboat race. "Those who know Flanagan," Marsh wrote, "know there isn't a crooked breath in his body."

What neither Flanagan nor Marsh mentioned until much later was that Flanagan didn't simply walk away from Longboat. He sold him. Flanagan had a contract with the runner, which called for a 50-50 split in his racing earnings, and Flanagan sold the contract to the New York promoter Pat Powers, for the not inconsiderable sum of $2,000.

Longboat was distraught at Flanagan's action. He may have recognized that Flanagan had been taking advantage of him in many ways, but Flanagan and his ICAC cronies had been constants in Longboat's life through most of his racing career. Without them, he felt lost. It was in this depressed state of mind, with Powers now calling the shots, that Longboat got ready to face Alf Shrubb in what was heating up to be the most anticipated race that Longboat had yet taken part in.

Shrubb was much the senior of the two runners at 35 years of age. He had worked as a stonemason in England, and didn't begin competitive running until he was 18. He was a trim man – five-foot-seven, 135 pounds – with a methodical style and a ferocious dedication to fitness. At one time, he held virtually all of the world amateur records for distances from two miles to ten.

Canada's Sports Hall of Fame

🐾 In this 1908 photograph, the young Longboat shows his confident form and his handsome looks.

Canada's Sports Hall of Fame

 In the early winter of 1908, when Longboat began to earn fair money as a professional racer, he sported fine clothes and enjoyed a good cigar.

In 1906, after Britain's amateur authorities learned that Shrubb had accepted a ticket from a Canadian friend to travel to races in Canada, he was declared a professional. The ruling made him ineligible for the London Olympics, but he developed a rewarding career by barnstorming around North America, running against all comers in professional races. He spent much time in Toronto, where he hung out at the Grand Central Hotel and where, beginning in the summer of 1907, he frequently and unsuccessfully challenged Longboat to high stakes races. He finally got what he was after when Powers booked the Madison Square Garden match — Shrubb versus Longboat at the marathon distance.

Longboat's training in New York went badly. He had one bright moment when he chased a thief down Sixth Avenue in Manhattan; the man had stolen a coat from a store on 31st Street, and when the storekeeper couldn't catch him, Longboat — who happened to be passing by — took over and nabbed the fleeing shoplifter at the end of a swift pursuit. Otherwise, Longboat seemed listless as he prepared for the race. It didn't help that the event had to be postponed a week when Shrubb came down with inflammation of his left big toe. Nor did Longboat much enjoy the intrusive press coverage, the equivalent in today's terms of the intense media buildup to a Super Bowl football game.

Longboat was so overwrought that, on January 26, he wrote a letter to Tim O'Rourke at the Grand Central. The letter began:

> *Dear friend,*
> *Just a few lines to let you know I am not in shape for this race, so I*
> *am just thinking of quitting the race before it gets too late. I think*
> *the next race puts me out of business. . . . I wouldn't bet a cent if I*
> *were you. I'm good for nothing now.*

Longboat intended the letter as a private communication, but O'Rourke turned the letter over to Marsh, who printed it in the *Star*. Longboat's despairing words were blown up in large type across the width of five columns on an inside news page.

Despite the letter's pessimism, Longboat took to the track at the Garden on the night of Saturday, February 6. If Longboat thought he had troubles with conditioning, Shrubb had a problem of his own. He had never run more than 15 miles in his career, and of the three 15-milers he had competed in, he lost all three – one of them to John Marsh in Winnipeg. This was a deficiency that Tom Flanagan, of all people, seized on. Even though Flanagan was officially out of the picture, his ego wouldn't allow him to stay away from such a prominent sporting event as the Longboat-Shrubb race. According to an article that Flanagan himself wrote in the *Toronto Telegram* on February 8, he predicted to Shrubb in a phone call the day before the race that Shrubb would never last more than 20 miles. Shrubb laughed at the prediction. But, Flanagan wrote, "the seed was sown." Then, as Flanagan bragged in the article, on the night of the race, he positioned himself in a spot at the side of the Garden track that put him in Shrubb's line of vision on each lap. "I took care that the Englishman saw me every time he came around," Flanagan wrote. "He knew I expected him to blow up at 20, and it must have been agony for him."

The Garden was filled for the race, and back in Toronto, thousands of people gathered in the streets around the *Star* building and Massey Hall. Both buildings displayed, outdoors, continuous up-to-the-minute reports direct from the track in New York. What the various audiences, in Toronto and in Madison Square Garden, caught on to instantly was Shrubb's strategy. He got away to a very fast start and maintained the quick pace through the following miles in the obvious expectation that he would wear down Longboat early and stick in front through the last miles for the win.

The strategy seemed to be brilliant. Shrubb ran the first mile in 4 minutes and 52 seconds. Longboat trailed in 5 minutes and 15 seconds. The difference gave Shrubb a lead of almost a half lap, and he kept building the advantage until, by the 20th mile, Shrubb was ahead by an astonishing four-fifths of a mile. He had lapped Longboat eight times. He was running so far in the lead that, barring catastrophe, he appeared a certain victor.

But in the 21st mile, the race began to turn ever so slightly. Shrubb showed the first signs of stress and fatigue. He stopped to take a long drink of water and to change his shoes. Before he set off again, Longboat had made up more than a lap. The new shoes briefly invigorated Shrubb before his stride slackened once again. Longboat appeared to have a golden opportunity to get back in the race, but the difficulty for Longboat, though his rival was suddenly vulnerable, was that he too was tired, and he still had a formidable margin to make up.

At the beginning of the 22nd mile, a man in suit and tie ran onto the track. It was Tom Flanagan. He couldn't resist the limelight. His prediction of Shrubb's collapse at 20 miles hadn't come true, but now he was on the track, ripping off his jacket and shirt, waving them over his head, trotting alongside Longboat and shouting at him to stay the course, that Shrubb was bound to give up soon.

Canada's Sports Hall of Fame

 In Longboat's 1909 match race against Alf Shrubb at Madison Square Garden in New York, Shrubb held a lead of almost eight laps. He began to falter late in the race and was forced to stop and change his shoes.

Three of Flanagan's sportsmen buddies joined him on the side of the track, yelling encouragement at Longboat. Shrubb fans in the Garden hooted at the Flanagan contingent, and Shrubb's trainers screamed at the Canadians to get back to their seats. The Garden was bedlam. And in the midst of the uproar, Shrubb slowed his pace to a hurried walk. His energy was deserting him. He walked through most of the 23rd and 24th miles, running only in spurts. Longboat ran steadily and cut into the lead. He wasn't making fast time – about seven minutes per mile – but it was quicker than the walking and staggering Shrubb. Four laps past the 25-mile mark, Longboat was less than a lap behind, and at that moment, Shrubb walked off the track in surrender to weariness. Longboat pushed himself through the last laps to the finish line and to triumph.

Before his thrilling race against Alf Shrubb at Madison Square Garden, Longboat poses with his trainer for the race, James Deforest; Hamilton, Ontario businessman Sol Mintz, who later became Longboat's manager; and his new wife, Lauretta.

The photograph on the front page of the following Monday's *Toronto Daily Star* showed a crowd of elated men carrying an equally rejoicing fellow on their shoulders. The man being held aloft had just stepped off the train from the big race in New York, and the crowd had turned out to celebrate him. The man was not Longboat. He was Tom Flanagan. "To Flanagan belongs the real credit of winning the race," Lou Marsh wrote, apparently reflecting the opinion among insiders in Toronto racing circles. "He worked like a hero and pulled a man through to victory who had but little real licence to win."

Longboat answered this insult to his gallant effort against Shrubb with a simple question: "Do you think Flanagan could make me run if I didn't want to?" With that off his chest, Longboat quietly took up domestic life with his wife, Lauretta. They rented a pleasant three-story redbrick house on Galley Avenue in the Parkdale section of west Toronto and settled in. Two years later, they would move a few blocks north and west to an even larger rented house on Pacific Avenue, in a more upscale neighborhood a half block above High Park. With Longboat's breakup from Flanagan, he was out of the cigar store business, which was assumed by an established Toronto tobacco merchant named Samuel Beernbohm. This left Longboat with plenty of free time to devote to life with Lauretta and to training.

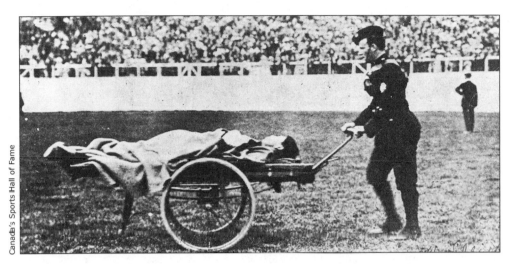

🥾 It was the blazing sun that forced Longboat out of the Chicago Marathon on a hot afternoon in July 1909.

🥾 Longboat's frequent rival, Alf Shrubb, accumulated trophies from victories all over North America, Great Britain, and Australia.

Unfortunately for Longboat's immediate racing career, he spent many more hours with the former than the latter. Pat Powers begged him to capitalize on his popularity by competing in match races in New York against a variety of opponents. But Longboat, happy in marital bliss and ignoring his conditioning regimen altogether, refused every race except one, and it turned out to be a disaster.

The event, over the marathon distance, took place on April 3 at the Polo Grounds — the New York Giants' baseball park — and featured six runners from five countries: Longboat, Shrubb, Dorando, John Hayes, a new young American whiz named Matt Maloney, and one relative unknown, Henri St. Ives — a Frenchman who worked as a chauffeur in London, England, and had recently won the Scottish Marathon. A crowd of 40,000 showed up in wet, miserable weather and watched as Longboat, the favorite but clearly not in shape for a long run, dropped out in the 20th mile. Shrubb failed to finish too, Dorando came in second, and to everybody's amazement, the winner was the unheralded chauffeur, St. Ives.

Pat Powers grew fed up with Longboat's attitude and sold his contract at the discount price of $700 to a Hamilton, Ontario businessman named Sol Mintz. Mintz was no stranger to Longboat. He had been one of the three overexcited Canadians who ran onto the track alongside Tom Flanagan at the Shrubb race in the Garden. The Mintz-Longboat team had rocky moments near the beginning of their relationship: Longboat keeled over from sunstroke during the Chicago Marathon that summer, and he also lost to Shrubb in a Montreal race at 15 miles, a distance that was more suited to Shrubb's abilities.

But Longboat demonstrated that his career was hardly on the decline in two sensational races. First, on June 21, over a mushy track at the Exposition Grounds in Buffalo, he ran a cleverly tactical 10-mile race against a local hero named Frank Nebrick and won with a blazing final sprint. A week later, Longboat took on Alf Shrubb once more. The race was a 20-miler,

City of Toronto Archives, SC 244 - 61.17

 As a celebrity around Toronto, Longboat frequently posed for photographs that had nothing to do with running. In this 1909 photo, he prepares to toboggan, with two young women, down the run at High Park near his home.

and it was staged at the stadium on Hanlan's Point at the western end of the islands in Toronto's bay. The stadium was home field for the Maple Leafs of baseball's International League and the site of boxing matches, lacrosse games, and track meets. As before in Longboat-Shrubb contests, Shrubb roared off to a dynamic start and lapped Longboat in the seventh mile. But Longboat's strength and endurance held him in the race. He never once faltered or slowed in the chase after Shrubb until it was Shrubb who yielded. He quit at 15 miles, and Longboat loped to the win.

Life was on another upswing for Longboat. He had money, enough that, with the help of donations from fans, he was able to build a two-story cinder-block house on the Six Nations for his mother and other relatives. It's probably true that Longboat would have prospered even more if Tom Flanagan had still been his manager. For all of Flanagan's self-promoting ways, he had the finesse and contacts in the racing world to pull off major events that attracted large crowds. On the other hand, distance racing seemed to be retreating slightly as a spectator sport, and it may have been that the running craze peaked with Longboat's spectacular races at Madison Square Garden against Dorando and Shrubb. Still, Longboat remained a powerful drawing card, and his career had promise of carrying him through many more lucrative seasons.

The next year, 1910, proved to be both up and down for Longboat. He won most of his races, but lost in two-man matches against Dorando in Pittsburgh and Shrubb in Boston. Then, in July 1911, he suffered a terrible humiliation away from racing. Toronto police picked him up in the street, unsteady and smelling of alcohol, and in court, the judge convicted him of drunkenness in a public place. The official punishment was mild – a suspended sentence – but the penalty in the community was severe: a week of scornful newspaper stories and a lifetime of snickering remarks about Longboat the drunken Indian.

Longboat was hardly an alcoholic. If he were, he could never have run so many wonderful races nor, in later life, held jobs in the workplace so consistently. But when he was offered a chance to hoist a few drinks in a bar, he wasn't likely to put up much resistance. A man named Frank Montour once placed Longboat's situation in perspective. Montour, in his 90s when he spoke in 1987, was a lifelong Six Nations resident and a Longboat friend from childhood. "We all took a drink," he said, speaking of Six Nations men in general. "Usually we curbed it. There were times when we might have had one or two too many, but it never did any damage or harm."

With Longboat, the temptation to overindulge was increased by his celebrity; whenever he entered a bar, everybody in the place competed for the privilege of buying a beer or a shot of whiskey for the great Tom. Longboat rarely had to pay for a drink, and while drinking may not have done much harm to his running, it wasn't kind to his reputation.

As if to show what a resilient athlete Longboat really was, within a month of the drunkenness conviction, he ran two of his mightiest races ever, both at the Hanlan's Point Stadium. The first, on August 14, matched him yet again against Shrubb at 12 miles, a distance that favored Shrubb. This time, while Shrubb held the lead for eight miles, Longboat didn't let him out of his sight and came on strong at the finish to win by a half lap. The second race, on August 28, also at 12 miles, featured four runners with splendid credentials: Longboat, Shrubb, Charles Hefferon – the South African who finished second in the Olympic marathon – and a rising English star named

City of Toronto Archives, SC 244 – Item 6042

 Longboat ran many of his professional races at the Hanlan's Point Stadium on the Toronto Islands. The stadium, which accommodated 10,000 fans, was the scene of lacrosse matches, boxing bouts, and home games for the Toronto Maple Leaf baseball team. Note the sign advertising what turned out to be a classic Longboat-Shrubb 12-mile race on August 12, 1911; Longboat triumphed.

A. E. Wood. It was a 12–mile race in front of 9,000 roaring spectators, a race in which each competitor took turns holding the lead. The young Wood stayed in front from mile 5 until deep into mile 12, when Longboat made his ultimate move in the race's final lap. The two battled down the stretch, with Longboat crossing the finish line no more than a foot and a half ahead of Wood. The winning time was 1 hour, 2 minutes, 32 and 2/5 seconds. It was the fastest 12 miles Longboat had ever run.

Canada's Sports Hall of Fame

🐢 The majority of these medals and trophies, displayed here circa 1912, were eventually lost or melted down. Few remain in public or private hands today.

Before the end of 1911, Longboat took over management of his career from Sol Mintz, and one of his first bookings carried him to Scotland in early 1912 for two races at Edinburgh's Powderhall Stadium. The early race, a marathon, went poorly when a sore knee forced Longboat to drop out after 15 miles. But a month later, in a 15-mile race against an elite field of Europeans, Longboat burned up the track in a time of 1:20:04:4, which constituted a new professional record for the distance.

Longboat remained in glorious form through the rest of the year, winning a string of races in North America, which included one that probably represented the most impressive display of pure speed in his entire career. This race was at 15 miles in the Hanlan's Point Stadium against three other runners: the ever-present Shrubb, A. E. Wood, and a young American named

Billy Queal, who held the U.S. records at 10 and 12 miles. The four men were billed as "the fastest quartet alive," and they set out in the race to live up to the description. It was a contest without much strategy and few tactics. Instead it was a running race at its most fundamental – speed against speed – and Longboat proved to be the fastest, winning in a time that eclipsed by almost two seconds the record he had set earlier in the year in Edinburgh.

Longboat may have been reaching the pinnacle of his running talents in 1912, but his timing couldn't have been worse. It was the year, 1912, when distance running took a pronounced dive in fan popularity. Longboat continued to compete, but not as frequently and not in front of such large crowds. Part of the reason for the sport's downturn was economic: a recession had set in, and sports fans hadn't as much money to spend on athletic diversions. But the final factor that put an effective end to distance running and to several other forms of entertainment, in fact, to many of the formerly accepted events of ordinary day-to-day life, came from Europe in 1913 and early 1914. Europe was a continent in tense struggle, and the tensions were about to explode into a conflict that would overwhelm the world with unprecedented bloodshed for more than four years.

CHAPTER NINE

War

The immediate event that set off a war more deadly and costly than any war before it was the assassination of Austrian Archduke Francis Ferdinand by Bosnian Serbs in Sarajevo on June 28, 1914. It was this murder that firmed up alliances and confirmed rivalries among the European countries that had been jockeying for power over the previous decades. By early August 1914, war had been declared in most of the continent's capitals. On one side were the Central Powers: principally Germany, the Austro-Hungarian Empire, and Turkey. Allied on the other side were France, Russia, and Britain. Italy eventually came in with the Allies. So, in the spring of 1917, did the United States.

Canada had no choice. As a member of the British Empire, its duty was to enter the war in the summer of 1914 in support of its mother country, England. Before World War I ended on November 11, 1918, Canada had committed almost 500,000 men to battle. One of them was Tom Longboat.

In January 1916, Longboat enlisted in the Canadian Army's 37th Haldimand Rifles. But a month later, Tom Flanagan once again stepped into Longboat's life and changed its direction. Flanagan and a Toronto lawyer friend named Dick Greer formed the 180th Battalion within the Canadian forces and recruited their pals around the city to join them. The unit acquired a new name that reflected its membership – the 180th Sportsmen's Battalion.

Greer, whose instant rank was lieutenant colonel, served as the Battalion's commanding officer. Flanagan was a captain and the paymaster. Among others, Lou Marsh signed up with the Sportsmen's and went on to a distinguished army career; he served in the front lines of battle in Europe and ended the war with the rank of major. Flanagan's expertise as a sports manager and promoter led to his appointment as the Canadian officer in charge of organizing athletic events for the entertainment of the troops, both in Canada and later overseas. And in this capacity, he arranged for Longboat's transfer to the Sportsmen's Battalion.

According to stories later circulated by Flanagan, Marsh, and Greer, Longboat spent most of his first year of the war in two activities: running races and getting into trouble. Sometimes, so the stories went, he managed to do both at the same time. Once, at a rally staged in Toronto's Riverdale Park as an occasion to recruit new troops, Longboat was matched in a three-mile race against a fit runner named Jim Corkery. Since Longboat wasn't in prime physical condition, Flanagan instructed Corkery to take it easy in the first two and a half miles, nurse Longboat along, and to run all out only in the last half mile, the best man winning. Corkery did as he was told, and the race ended in a dead heat. The Duke of Connaught, Canada's governor-general at the time, was at the rally, and when he presented the prizes after the race, he asked Longboat in front of the assembled officers: "Was that dead heat honest?"

"Say," Longboat was supposed to have answered, "you're not as big a fool as they thought you were."

Longboat had difficulty adapting to military discipline. As a professional runner for his entire adult life, he had never before found himself in a structured work situation for any length of time. His days at W. J. Gage & Co. and in the cigar store hadn't made many demands of him, and the army was a tough place to start accepting formal authority. Longboat was the square peg in the round hole. He didn't fit, and he lacked the background and education to make an easy adjustment to the 180th Battalion's rules and regulations.

Nor did Longboat, who remained remarkably naive for a man close to thirty, show much judgment in choosing his army companions. Many soldiers were so delighted to discover themselves serving alongside the famous runner that they stroked their own egos by tempting the easily led Longboat into mischief. On one occasion, when the soldiers of the 180th were given the simple assignment of holding back the crowds while the 75th Battalion boarded a train at Riverdale Station in Toronto for the trip to Halifax and embarkation to Britain, some of the 75th's men poured Longboat a couple of drinks and coaxed him onto the train. Longboat didn't surface until three days later in Halifax.

Lieutenant Colonel Dick Greer said after the war that he frequently bailed Longboat out of the disciplinary jams he got himself into. Still, Longboat seems to have spent more than his share of days doing fatigue duty, cleaning out latrines, and performing other lowly chores as punishment for his offences. He enjoyed representing the Sportsmen's in running competitions against other battalions, invariably finishing in the top two or three, but the rest of the time, he was largely unsuccessful at coping with army life.

After one race, Longboat was presented to His Majesty, King George V of England and the British Empire.

"Private Longboat," the king said, "please tell me if there is any way I might oblige you."

"Yes," Longboat apparently answered, "get me out of here and let me go home to my mother."

In January 1917, everything changed for Longboat. That month, now posted overseas, he went into battle. But it wasn't with the 180th Sportsmen's. It was with the 197th, a battalion composed almost entirely of Canadian Indians. Before the war was over, Longboat was moved among three or four different military groups. With all of them, he was assigned to the same duty, a role that demanded his particular talent: Longboat was an army runner.

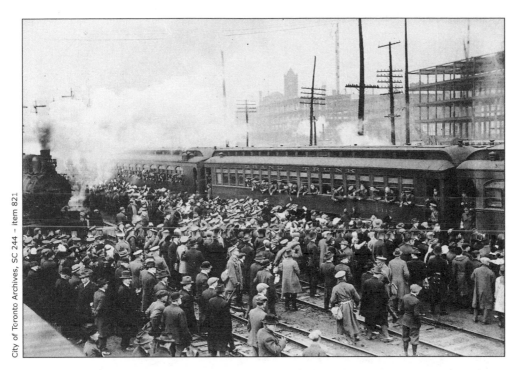

👟 Longboat went overseas in World War I with the 180th Sportsmen's Battalion, shown here leaving Toronto for Halifax in 1916. From Halifax, it embarked for Britain and eventual service at the front.

👟 Longboat joined the Canadian Army in 1916 to fight in World War I, but spent part of his time competing in races for the entertainment of his fellow soldiers.

In World War I, Longboat served as an army runner, carrying messages to the front lines. In this photo Longboat, on the right, takes time out from the war to buy an English-language newspaper from a French newsboy.

His job was to carry messages from one headquarters to another, from command posts behind the lines to other posts in the thick of the fighting. When two points could not maintain contact through radio, the runner replaced the failed electronic communication. It was a task with a high degree of danger, taking the runner close to the firing lines, over ground that was open to bombardment from enemy guns, vulnerable to shells and whizzing bullets. By all accounts, Longboat carried out his duties with distinction and valor. He worked close to two of the most terrible battles that Canadians fought: Vimy Ridge in April 1917 and Passchendaele near the end of the same year. Though both were regarded as victories, thousands of Canadians gave their lives in the two battles. Longboat was one of the brave and fortunate survivors.

He experienced more than a few frights. After the war he said that the first time a big bomb whined over his head, "I never thought I'd see Canada again." He suffered no wounds in battle, barely a scratch, though many stories circulated that Longboat got buried more than once in trenches that had been hit by shells. The most often-repeated Longboat adventure was that he and some other men had been stuck underground for six whole days. The story, as was much about Longboat's wartime experience, turned out not to be accurate. Longboat himself debunked the account of the six-day burial in an interview he gave Lou Marsh when both men returned to Canada in 1919. Marsh asked Longboat if he had ever been caught underground during the fighting. "Nope," Longboat answered. "Just splattered with mud and knocked down." But the denial didn't prevent the false tale of Longboat's six days in a trench from being repeated in all the subsequent writings about his life.

What is not to be questioned was that Longboat was mistakenly reported killed in action on at least two occasions. This was the sort of bureaucratic error that occurred frequently in the chaos of World War I. Hundreds of soldiers whom the Canadian Army simply lost track of ended up on lists of those killed in action. Back home in Canada, soldiers' wives were left with the impression that they had become widows. Many of them took up with other men. That was apparently the case with Lauretta Longboat. In fact, according to an often repeated story, thinking Tom was dead, Lauretta married another man.

In later years, this was the version of events that Longboat's children by his second marriage accepted. "There was a rumor he had been killed in action," Tom Longboat Jr. said of his father in 1987. "When he got home, he found out his wife had married another man. He was pretty mad, he could have killed her, I guess, but people told him not to bother about her. So then he went with my mother."

But the story of Lauretta and the other man may not be true. As late as 1920 – a year after Longboat got back from overseas – Lauretta was listed in the Toronto telephone directory as LAURETTA LONGBOAT at 718 SPADINA AVENUE. When she died in August 1952 at age 71, an obituary notice referred to her as Lauretta Maracle and her place of death as the town of Oshwegan on the Six Nations. The small available evidence suggests that Lauretta may never have remarried and may even have reclaimed her maiden name. (Her death left another mystery. The obituary said that she was survived by a son, Reginald Longboat. Was Tom the father of Reginald? It appears likely, but in all the literature about Longboat, in all of his recorded conversations, there is reference only to the four children of his second marriage, none of them named Reginald.)

If it's unclear whether Longboat and Lauretta ended their marriage by divorce, by annulment, or through some sort of legislative directive arising out of the peculiar circumstances of the war, it's certain that Longboat was left free to remarry. His second wife, whom he married in 1920, was named Martha Silversmith, a Seneca from the Six Nations reserve. Like everybody else on the Six Nations, Martha had been a Tom Longboat fan for years. She had often travelled with her friends to Buffalo and Hamilton to cheer him on in his races. One writer of the time described Martha as "a slim woman of Tom's age, soft-spoken and courteous." She seems not to have been the beauty that Lauretta was, but she and Longboat suited one another so well that they remained together for the rest of Longboat's life.

Before he got on with his new marriage and with a career away from running, Longboat had a few more good races left in him. Unfortunately, the professional racing circuit had all but vanished. Other sports had stepped up in popularity, mostly team games – baseball and hockey in particular. Still, Longboat, now in his early thirties, had a handful of opportunities to demonstrate that he retained the stuff of the great racer he had always been.

Perhaps the race most characteristic of the old Longboat took place on the night of July 18, 1919, at the venue where Longboat had flourished in the past – the Hanlan's Point Stadium. The event was called the Grand Army of Canada Show, and it attracted a crowd of 4,000, who were treated to a boxing card and a three-mile match race between Longboat and an opponent from pre-war days, Billy Queal, the former American record holder.

The race was a thriller. Longboat held the lead for most of the three miles and was 75 yards in front of Queal, with just a quarter of a mile to go. He looked a sure winner, but the younger Queal closed the gap with such a rush that, twenty yards from the finish line, the two men were neck and neck. Longboat could have given in to Queal's incredible charge, but he rallied himself, and in the flat-out run to the tape, he beat Queal by a foot.

Longboat walked away from the last great race of his life engulfed once again in the cheers of an adoring crowd.

CHAPTER TEN

His Own Man

Longboat went west. He decided that he and his wife, Martha, should begin their new life together by working a farm of their own in Alberta. The federal government had set up a program of land grants for men who had served in the recent war. But somehow, out west, when Longboat applied for land, errors in paperwork and bureaucratic foul-ups prevented him from taking up his grant. He hired on as a hand on someone else's farm near Edmonton and later moved into the city, where he got a job as a shipper in a warehouse.

Longboat had no savings to fall back on. According to one reporter's version, Longboat's earnings from his racing career vanished in "liquor, fancy clothes and foolish investments in real estate." It's possible that alcohol accounted for some of Longboat's financial losses, though, as we've seen, he rarely had to pay for his own drinks. Photographs of Longboat during his running days show him to have been a stylish dresser who favored bowler hats, high-collared shirts, and smartly tailored suits. Such clothes wouldn't have been cheap. As for the real estate investments, these have never been documented, apart from the house on the Six Nations that Longboat built for his mother and hung on to until his own death. Whatever happened to Longboat's money – whether or not sharp operators on the sporting scene helped to separate him from it – the fact was, by the early 1920s, that Longboat found himself broke.

Canada's Sports Hall of Fame

In this photograph, probably taken in the 1920s after his retirement, Longboat looks fit and dapper.

Martha Longboat didn't care for life in Edmonton. It was too far from the comfort of the familiar landscape and the old friends on the Six Nations. And she disliked the idea of raising her children in the West. The first Longboat child, a daughter named Winnie, was born in 1921, and she was eventually followed by Teddy in 1923, Tom Jr. in 1925, and Clifford in 1927. Not long after Winnie's birth, Longboat agreed with Martha's wish to move back east, and in October 1922, the penniless Longboat family arrived in Toronto.

Longboat appealed to Flanagan for help. Flanagan treated him to a meal of corned beef and cabbage at the Grand Central Hotel and made a phone call to a pal on Longboat's behalf. The call landed Longboat a laborer's job at the Dunlop Rubber Company in west Toronto at a salary of three dollars a day. Flanagan's act showed him at his most generous, but the man's mean-spirited side revealed itself when he provided Lou Marsh with information to help Marsh write the long article that appeared a month later in the *Star Weekly* subjecting Longboat to scorn and ridicule.

Marsh stated his familiar theme early in the article: "[Longboat] started on corn pone, worked up to caviar and now is tickled to get corn beef regularly." As he often had in the past, Marsh portrayed Longboat as a foolish Indian who should have listened to his white betters. He listed errors that Longboat supposedly made in his running career, in his training habits; he referred to his misbehavior in the army, his failure to think in a businesslike manner. Many of Marsh's criticisms had validity, but the article, in its pitiless contempt, amounted to a case of kicking a man when he was down.

Longboat was destined to fall even further. One day, while he was at work on the floor of the Dunlop Rubber Company, a piece of heavy metal dropped on Longboat's left foot. It crushed one of his toes. He was in agony. He couldn't walk. The company doctor told him the toe would have to be amputated. Longboat asked for other opinions, but the other doctors gave the same advice. The toe was useless; it must be removed.

Longboat decided not to accept their diagnosis. Instead, he followed a path that reflected a change in his thinking and attitude. He rejected the white doctors' counsel and returned to the Indian wisdom he grew up with on the Six Nations. It was both a medical and a spiritual decision, and it marked a turning point in Longboat's life. He had paid little attention to the Anglican faith that Lauretta Maracle had introduced him to. He hadn't taken an active role in the Onondaga religion either. But now, in the crisis over his health, he went back to the Six Nations and consulted one of the holy men on the reserve.

The man was a medicine man. He mixed a potion and wrapped it in a healing balm around Longboat's foot. Three weeks later, Longboat could walk again. Within another month, the toe returned to its normal state. Longboat's body was cured, and at the same time, his confidence was buoyed. He grew settled in himself. He began to adjust to the demands of the more modest life he was leading in the aftermath of his great fame.

The visit to the medicine man was far from the last that Longboat made. A year after the episode over the crushed toe, Longboat's first son, Teddy, was born. The baby was sickly. Doctors couldn't find the source of the illness. Teddy grew worse, and the doctors told Longboat the little boy was fatally ill. Again, Longboat rejected their opinion and took his son to a medicine man on the Six Nations. This medicine man said the case was too complex for him and referred Longboat to another medicine man in Upper New York State. The New York man concocted a potion, fed it to the baby, and in a matter of days, Teddy began a recovery to full health.

In the mid-1920s, Longboat worked in steel mills in Hamilton and Buffalo, then returned to Toronto in 1927, where he found employment with the city of Toronto in its Street Cleaning Department – a job he held until 1944. He drove horse-drawn carts, and later motor trucks, around the streets, sweeping up leaves and refuse, keeping the roads clean and tidy. For some scoffing Canadians, the job represented Longboat's ultimate comedown. "Literally," a long article in the February 4, 1956 *Maclean's* magazine typically summed up, "[Longboat's] was a story of Public Hero to Garbage Collector." What the scoffers overlooked was, while Longboat's occupation was undeniably humble, that he remained employed through the terrible years of the 1930s Depression when many Torontonians lost their jobs, their homes, and their hope. Longboat had a regular salary, and in the hard times, he supported his family in comfort and safety.

"We always dressed well," Tom Jr. recalled in 1987, speaking of his child-hood. "We always lived in a nice house."

Longboat continued to enjoy popularity among men and women who remembered his glory years. He was an annual guest at the Hamilton Around the Bay Race, and he took part in exhibition runs himself. The city of Hamilton staged a four-mile race for old-timers as part of its 1927 Diamond Jubilee celebrations. Bill Sherring was an entrant, along with many other champion runners of the past. Longboat agreed to enter on the condition that the winner receive a car as first prize. Not necessarily a new sedan, Longboat said; something secondhand would do. Longboat won the race with a brilliant final sprint, and for years, he drove his family in style in the fine secondhand automobile.

In 1930, Longboat experienced a difficult period. That summer brought his final significant race: a one-mile run at the Canadian National Exhibition against his old-time rival Alf Shrubb. Shrubb won easily. But worse came two months later when Longboat was crippled by severe back pain. Tom felt certain that the cause of his trouble was an enemy on the Six Nations who had called on evil spirits to lay a curse on him. A Six Nations medicine man, who confirmed Longboat's belief, sent him to another medicine man in Gowanda, New York, and it was this second man who prepared the power-ful medicine that expelled the curse. The curing process took much longer than the twenty-four days that the Street Cleaning Department allowed its employees for medical leave, but the department, apparently accepting the unorthodox origins of Longboat's ailment and of the ailment's cure, kept his job open for him. In mid-November 1930, Longboat went back to work, free of pain.

Jack Batten

👟 Even though Longboat made his living as a street cleaner after his racing career ended, he and his family lived in fine houses in Toronto, including (in 1934 and 1935) this home at 229 Erskine Avenue in North Toronto.

Through the 1930s and early 1940s, Longboat and his family lived in a succession of eight rented homes in Lawrence Park and other neighborhoods in Toronto's prosperous north end. All of the houses were roomy and comfortable, with good schools nearby. For two years, 1934–35, their home was at 229 Erskine Avenue, a charming corner house on a virtually traffic-free stretch that dead-ended at a leafy ravine; four decades later, Claude Bissell, president of the University of Toronto from 1958 to 1971, bought the house and lived in it for 29 years until his death in 2000.

An even more impressive Longboat home, and the one the family occupied the longest, from 1939 to 1944, was at 126 Roslin, a two-story detached house close to the Don Valley and just south of the exclusive Rosedale Golf Club. Longboat lived well, though within his limited means, and he was generous with his home and his hospitality. "His house was open for everybody from the reserve," said Frank Montour, Longboat's childhood friend, "and you could expect a good time there."

Longboat still suffered occasional heartbreaks. In August 1932, he was driving his family home from a visit to the Canadian National Exhibition. He stopped at a radio station on north Yonge Street, and left the children in the car while he did a commercial with a woman named Jane Grey, who hosted a program under the fake Indian name of Princess Mus-Kee-Kee, which was also the name of a patent medicine. When Longboat came out of the radio station, his youngest son, Clifford, only five years old, darted onto Yonge Street to greet his daddy. A woman at the wheel of a passing car was unable to stop in time to avoid the little boy. Her car struck and killed Clifford.

"I think it was the saddest day of my parents' lives," Tom Jr. said many years later.

On July 7, 1935, another automobile brought grief to Longboat. This time it was his own car. He was driving it on a holiday trip to the Six Nations when the Caledonia police pulled him over. Longboat was drunk. The judge sentenced him to a week in the local jail. The only consolation Longboat found in the embarrassing event, he said later, was that his sentence came during weed-cutting week for the prisoners. That meant Longboat spent his sentence outdoors in fresh air.

The following year, on March 4, 1936, Lou Marsh, aged 59, died after a stroke. The *Star* gave his death a coverage that might have seemed excessive if it had been reporting the death of a prime minister. The front page headline announced in large type: LOU E. MARSH, STAR SPORTS EDITOR, PASSES. Under it, there appeared a three-column-wide photograph of Marsh, along with four front page stories about him, followed by five more pages of accounts on the inside. The articles included quotes of lavish praise from politicians and athletes, sportsmen and fellow writers, and among them were a few words from Longboat. "Lou Marsh was one of the finest men I ever knew," Longboat said. "He never forgot a friend."

Was Longboat unaware that Marsh had consistently insulted and criticized him in the *Star*? Given Longboat's artless nature, that is more than possible. Or were Longboat's final words simply the product of his character as a good-hearted man who had a warm word for everyone, even Lou Marsh? That, too, makes a believable explanation for the generous parting quote about the man who had hardly earned a description as Longboat's "friend."

By the early 1940s, Longboat's satisfaction with life in Toronto was diminishing. The house on Roslin was empty of children. Winnie had married, and both boys – Teddy and Tom Jr. – had joined the armed services to do their duty in World War II. Longboat continued to work for the Street Cleaning Department, but his back pains once again flared up, though there was no mention this time of a curse from a Six Nations rival. He was also suffering from the effects of diabetes.

In late 1944, Longboat left his city job, and he and Martha moved to the Six Nations, where they settled in a small, plain house. For a short period, Longboat served as a guard at the Canadian Army's former No. 20 Camp on Six Nations land, but eventually the diabetes put him in complete retirement. He passed his days in long walks, in conversations with old Six Nations friends, and in taking care of one piece of business that had been bothering him for years.

Throughout his career, Longboat had been plagued by men who passed themselves off in bars as "Tom Longboat" in order to coax free drinks from gullible patrons. These impostors were partly responsible for Longboat's reputation as a heavy drinker, and the worst offender of all continued to operate in the Hamilton area at the time of Longboat's retirement.

"This man has been capitalizing on my famous name for the last fifteen or twenty years," Longboat wrote in a letter to the *Hamilton Spectator*, "and I think it's high time I put a stop to it once and for all."

The letter drew widespread publicity. Bill Sherring was one of many who spoke up on Longboat's behalf. "Tom Longboat is a perfect gentleman and the soul of honor," Sherring told the *Spectator*. Everybody agreed that Longboat's name had been unfairly tarnished, and with the spread of his complaint, the Hamilton impostor was at last driven out of his nasty business.

Toward the end of 1948, Longboat's health began to desert him. The steady deterioration, largely brought on by his diabetes, ended his long walks and confined him to home. He soon developed pneumonia, and it was from this that he died on January 9, 1949.

His death attracted respectful stories in the Toronto newspapers, though they were nothing close to the intense coverage that he received at the height of his running career. Few of Longboat's friends from the glory days attended his funeral – Bill Sherring and one of Tom's former managers, Sol Mintz, showed up – but the ceremony itself, carried out in traditional Onondaga form and language in the Onondaga longhouse, drew a large crowd of Six Nations mourners.

Following the centuries-old custom, Onondaga women prepared burial clothing for Longboat that was entirely hand-stitched, without pins or buttons. His body was placed in a simple coffin with a V-shaped notch cut into one end to allow his spirit to escape and join the spirits of his ancestors. The coffin was then put to rest in a burial ground in the woods close by the Onondaga longhouse. The grave remains secluded to this day, visited only on the occasion of funerals of other Onondagas and on the two days each year when people of the Six Nations clean and honor the burial ground.

Longboat left behind almost nothing in his own possessions that reflected his remarkable running feats. During his financially distressed period in Edmonton in the early 1920s, he pawned sixteen of the valuable medals he had won in races all over North America. An Edmonton lawyer named Moe Lieberman retrieved most of the medals and kept them for future purchase by collectors. But when no collectors appeared, the medals were apparently melted and sold as bulk metal. The single Longboat award on public display today, perhaps the only significant award that has survived intact, is a large and ornate trophy marking one of Longboat's victories in the Ward Marathon. The trophy, looking alone and forlorn, sits in the museum at the Woodland Cultural Centre on the Six Nations.

One Longboat legacy that had been overlooked for decades surfaced in 1979 when Bruce Kidd brought it to light. Kidd was a champion runner at the middle and long distances in the 1960s and '70s, and it was he who discovered that the $500 granted to Longboat by the city of Toronto in recognition of his win in the 1907 Boston Marathon continued to sit in a city bank account. He reasoned that the original $500 was worth $14,500 in 1979 money, and he developed a plan for the cash. It should go to the National Indian Brotherhood to establish, in Longboat's name, scholarships for young Native athletes.

Kidd took the idea to his old high school friend at Toronto's Malvern Collegiate, John Sewell, who happened then to be Toronto's mayor. Sewell thought a reduced figure – $10,000 – would stand a better chance of getting through a council vote, and on February 18, 1980, he put a motion before council that would release Longboat's 1907 money, in the updated sum of $10,000, to the National Indian Brotherhood for athletic scholarships.

The *Toronto Sun* had other ideas: it championed the cause of Longboat's heirs – the three children – as the rightful recipients of the $10,000. When Sewell's motion came to a vote of council on March 31, the *Sun*'s counter-proposal carried the day by a conclusive majority of 19-4. Later in 1980, Winnie, Teddy, and Tom Jr., all getting on in years and in need of financial aid, divided the money that originated in their father's great victory of 1907.

Over the years, Longboat's achievements have come to be recognized in the low-key manner that Canada often uses to honor its former heroes. A plaque memorializing his running feats was unveiled in Oshwegan on the Six Nations. A junior high school in Toronto took Longboat's name. So did a four-block-long Toronto street and a running club for young people. And in a 1998 issue of *Maclean's* magazine that saluted "The 100 Most Important Canadians in History," Longboat appeared at the top of the ten-person category called Stars, ahead of Wayne Gretzky (third place), Marshall McLuhan (fifth), and Céline Dion (ninth).

Toronto Star

One of the few places where Longboat's feats are still recalled today is on this plaque unveiled on the Six Nations reserve in the summer of 1985 by MP Bud Bradley and Longboat's son, Tom Jr.

Longboat was a "star" in the running firmament. When he ran, he shone. He attracted light, and he gave it off, back to his fans and admirers around the world. He grew up poor and underclass, a Native, and he remained shy and not entirely at ease in white society for much of his life. But in his long moment of glory, when he ran against other men and against the record book, one truth became clear: Tom Longboat was the man who ran faster than everyone.

Acknowledgments

The following people and institutions were exceptionally generous in providing research material, photographs, and support. The City of Toronto Archives. The Ontario Archives. The National Archives. The Bata Shoe Museum. Canada's Sports Hall of Fame and its executive director, Allan Stewart. The *Toronto Star*, specifically Dan Smith. The *Globe and Mail*, specifically Sheree-Lee Olson. The Toronto Public Library, especially the Spadina Road branch and the Toronto Reference Library. The Anglican Church of Canada. Bob McMullan. Coleen Quinn, who tracked Internet sources. Mike Filey. John Sewell. Bruce Kidd. John Sebert. And, last but never least, Marjorie Harris.

Index